Getting Started with
Microsoft® Office

FrontPage® 2003

GRETCHEN
MARX
Saint Joseph College

PEARSON
Prentice
Hall

**Upper Saddle River
New Jersey 07458**

Library of Congress Cataloging-in-Publication Data

Marx, Gretchen.
   Getting started with Microsoft Office FrontPage 2003 / Gretchen Marx.
       p. cm. -- (The exploring Office series)
   Includes index.
   ISBN 0-13-143485-3
   1. Microsoft FrontPage. 2. Web sites--Design. 3. Web publishing. I. Title. II. Series.

TK5105.8885.F76M36 2004
005.7'2--dc22   2004044388

Executive Acquisitions Editor: Jodi McPherson
VP/ Publisher: Natalie E. Anderson
Associate Director of IT Product Development: Melonie Salvati
Senior Project Manager, Editorial: Eileen Clark
Editorial Assistants: Jodi Bolognese and Jasmine Slowik
Media Project Manager: Cathleen Profitko
Marketing Manager: Emily Williams Knight
Marketing Assistant: Nicole Beaudry
Production Manager: Gail Steier de Acevedo
Project Manager, Production: Lynne Breitfeller
Production Editor: Greg Hubit
Associate Director, Manufacturing: Vincent Scelta
Manufacturing Buyer: Lynne Breitfeller
Design Manager: Maria Lange
Interior Design: Michael J. Fruhbeis
Cover Design: Michael J. Fruhbeis
Cover Printer: Phoenix Color
Composition and Project Management: The GTS Companies
Printer/ Binder: Banta Menasha

10 9
ISBN 0-13-143485-3

To Barret, Jeremy, and Elliot —
you are the meaning of life

Gretchen Marx

Contents

MICROSOFT® OFFICE **FRONTPAGE® 2003**

Creating a Web Site: Introduction to Microsoft® Office FrontPage® 2003   1

Preface

Continuing a tradition of excellence, Prentice Hall is proud to announce the new *Exploring Microsoft Office 2003* series by Robert T. Grauer and Maryann Barber. The hands-on approach and conceptual framework of this comprehensive series helps students master all aspects of the Microsoft Office 2003 software, while providing the background necessary to transfer and use these skills in their personal and professional lives.

The entire series has been revised to include the new features found in the Office 2003 Suite, which contains Word 2003, Excel 2003, Access 2003, PowerPoint 2003, Publisher 2003, FrontPage 2003, and Outlook 2003.

In addition, this edition includes fully revised end-of-chapter material that provides an extensive review of concepts and techniques discussed in the chapter. Each chapter now begins with an *introductory case study* to provide an effective overview of what the reader will be able to accomplish, with additional *mini cases* at the end of each chapter for practice and review. The conceptual content within each chapter has been modified as appropriate and numerous end-of-chapter exercises have been added.

The new *visual design* introduces the concept of *perfect pages*, whereby every step in every hands-on exercise, as well as every end-of-chapter exercise, begins at the top of its own page and has its own screen shot. This clean design allows for easy navigation throughout the text.

Continuing the success of the website provided for previous editions of this series, Exploring Office 2003 offers expanded resources that include online, interactive study guides, data file downloads, technology updates, additional case studies and exercises, and other helpful information. Start out at www.prenhall.com/grauer to explore these resources!

Organization of the Exploring Office 2003 Series

The new Exploring Microsoft Office 2003 series includes four combined Office 2003 texts from which to choose:

- **Volume I** is Microsoft Office Specialist certified in each of the core applications in the Office suite (Word, Excel, Access, and PowerPoint). Five additional modules (*Essential Computing Concepts, Getting Started with Windows XP, The Internet and the World Wide Web, Getting Started with Outlook,* and *Integrated Case Studies*) are also included.

- **Volume II** picks up where Volume I leaves off, covering the advanced topics for the individual applications. A *Getting Started with VBA* module has been added.

- The **Brief Microsoft Office 2003** edition provides less coverage of the core applications than Volume I (a total of 10 chapters as opposed to 18). It also includes the *Getting Started with Windows XP* and *Getting Started with Outlook* modules.

- **Getting Started with Office 2003** contains the first chapter from each application (Word, Excel, Access, and PowerPoint), plus three additional modules: *Getting Started with Windows XP, The Internet and the World Wide Web,* and *Essential Computing Concepts.*

Individual texts for Word 2003, Excel 2003, Access 2003, and PowerPoint 2003 provide complete coverage of the application and are Microsoft Office Specialist certified. For shorter courses, we have created brief versions of the Exploring texts that give students a four-chapter introduction to each application. Each of these volumes is Microsoft Office Specialist certified at the Specialist level.

This series has been approved by Microsoft to be used in preparation for Microsoft Office Specialist exams.

The Microsoft Office Specialist program is globally recognized as the standard for demonstrating desktop skills with the Microsoft Office suite of business productivity applications (Microsoft Word, Microsoft Excel, Microsoft PowerPoint, Microsoft Access, and Microsoft Outlook). With a Microsoft Office Specialist certification, thousands of people have demonstrated increased productivity and have proved their ability to utilize the advanced functionality of these Microsoft applications.

By encouraging individuals to develop advanced skills with Microsoft's leading business desktop software, the Microsoft Office Specialist program helps fill the demand for qualified, knowledgeable people in the modern workplace. At the same time, Microsoft Office Specialist helps satisfy an organization's need for a qualitative assessment of employee skills.

Instructor and Student Resources

The **Instructor's CD** that accompanies the Exploring Office series contains:

- Student data files
- Solutions to all exercises and problems
- PowerPoint lectures
- Instructor's manuals in Word format that enable the instructor to annotate portions of the instructor manuals for distribution to the class

■ Instructors may also use our *test creation software*, TestGen and QuizMaster.

TestGen is a test generator program that lets you view and easily edit testbank questions, transfer them to tests, and print in a variety of formats suitable to your teaching situation. The program also offers many options for organizing and displaying testbanks and tests. A random number test generator enables you to create multiple versions of an exam.

QuizMaster, also included in this package, allows students to take tests created with TestGen on a local area network. The QuizMaster Utility built into TestGen lets instructors view student records and print a variety of reports. Building tests is easy with TestGen, and exams can be easily uploaded into WebCT, BlackBoard, and CourseCompass.

Prentice Hall's Companion Website at www.prenhall.com/grauer offers expanded IT resources and downloadable supplements. This site also includes an online study guide for students containing true/false and multiple choice questions and practice projects.

WebCT www.prenhall.com/webct

Gold level customer support available exclusively to adopters of Prentice Hall courses is provided free-of-charge upon adoption and provides you with priority assistance, training discounts, and dedicated technical support.

Blackboard www.prenhall.com/blackboard

Prentice Hall's abundant online content, combined with Blackboard's popular tools and interface, result in robust Web-based courses that are easy to implement, manage, and use—taking your courses to new heights in student interaction and learning.

CourseCompass www.coursecompass.com

CourseCompass is a dynamic, interactive online course management tool powered by Blackboard. This exciting product allows you to teach with marketing-leading Pearson Education content in an easy-to-use, customizable format.

Training and Assessment www2.phgenit.com/support

Prentice Hall offers Performance Based Training and Assessment in one product, Train&Assess IT. The Training component offers computer-based training that a student can use to preview, learn, and review Microsoft Office application skills. Web or CD-ROM delivered, Train IT offers interactive multimedia, computer-based training to augment classroom learning. Built-in prescriptive testing suggests a study path based not only on student test results but also on the specific textbook chosen for the course.

The Assessment component offers computer-based testing that shares the same user interface as Train IT and is used to evaluate a student's knowledge about specific topics in Word, Excel, Access, PowerPoint, Windows, Outlook, and the Internet. It does this in a task-oriented, performance-based environment to demonstrate proficiency as well as comprehension on the topics by the students. More extensive than the testing in Train IT, Assess IT offers more administrative features for the instructor and additional questions for the student.

Assess IT also allows professors to test students out of a course, place students in appropriate courses, and evaluate skill sets.

OPENING CASE STUDY

New! Each chapter now begins with an introductory case study to provide an effective overview of what students will accomplish by completing the chapter.

CHAPTER

1

Getting Started with Microsoft® Windows® XP

OBJECTIVES

After reading this chapter you will:

1. Describe the Windows desktop.
2. Use the Help and Support Center to obtain information.
3. Describe the My Computer and My Documents folders.
4. Differentiate between a program file and a data file.
5. Download a file from the Exploring Office Web site.
6. Copy and/or move a file from one folder to another.
7. Delete a file, and then recover it from the Recycle Bin.
8. Create and arrange shortcuts on the desktop.
9. Use the Search Companion.
10. Use the My Pictures and My Music folders.
11. Use Windows Messenger for instant messaging.

hands-on exercises

1. WELCOME TO WINDOWS XP
   Input: None
   Output: None

2. DOWNLOAD PRACTICE FILES
   Input: Data files from the Web
   Output: Welcome to Windows XP (a Word document)

3. WINDOWS EXPLORER
   Input: Data files from exercise 2
   Output: Screen Capture within a Word document

4. INCREASING PRODUCTIVITY
   Input: Data files from exercise 3
   Output: None

5. FUN WITH WINDOWS XP
   Input: None
   Output: None

CASE STUDY
UNFORESEEN CIRCUMSTANCES

Steve and his wife Shelly have poured their life savings into the dream of owning their own business, a "nanny" service agency. **They have spent the last two** years building their business and have created a sophisticated database with numerous entries for both families and nannies. The database is the key to their operation. Now that it is up and running, Steve and Shelly are finally at a point where they could hire someone to manage the operation on a part-time basis so that they could take some time off together.

Unfortunately, their process for selecting a person they could trust with their business was not as thorough as it should have been. Nancy, their new employee, assured them that all was well, and the couple left for an extended weekend. The place was in shambles on their return. Nancy could not handle the responsibility, and when Steve gave her two weeks' notice, neither he nor his wife thought that the unimaginable would happen. On her last day in the office Nancy "lost" all of the names in the database—the data was completely gone!

Nancy claimed that a "virus" knocked out the database, but after spending nearly $1,500 with a computer consultant, Steve was told that it had been cleverly deleted from the hard drive and could not be recovered. Of course, the consultant asked Steve and Shelly about their backup strategy, which they sheepishly admitted did not exist. They had never experienced any problems in the past, and simply assumed that their data was safe. Fortunately, they do have hard copy of the data in the form of various reports that were printed throughout the time they were in business. They have no choice but to manually reenter the data. ■

Your assignment is to read the chapter, paying special attention to the information on file management. Think about how Steve and Shelly could have avoided the disaster if a backup strategy had been in place, then summarize your thoughts in a brief note to your instructor. Describe the elements of a basic backup strategy. Give several other examples of unforeseen circumstances that can cause data to be lost.

1

New! A listing of the input and output files for each hands-on exercise within the chapter. Students will stay on track with what is to be accomplished.

PERFECT PAGES

Each step in the hands-on exercises begins at the top of the page to ensure that students can easily navigate through the text.

hands-on exercise

1   Welcome to Windows XP

Objective   To log on to Windows XP and customize the desktop; to open the My Computer folder; to move and size a window; to format a floppy disk and access the Help and Support Center. Use Figure 7 as a guide.

Step 1:   **Log On to Windows XP**

■ Turn on the computer and all of the peripheral devices. The floppy drive should be empty prior to starting your machine.

■ Windows XP will load automatically, and you should see a login screen similar to Figure 7a. (It does not matter which version of Windows XP you are using.) The number and names of the potential users and their associated icons will be different on your system.

■ Click the icon for the user account you want to access. You may be prompted for a password, depending on the security options in effect.

Click icon for user account to be accessed

(a) Log On to Windows XP (step 1)

FIGURE 7   Hands-on Exercise 1

USER ACCOUNTS

The available user names are cr
Windows XP, but you can add or d
click Control Panel, switch to the Ca
the desired task, such as creating
then supply the necessary informati
user accounts in a school setting.

10   GETTING STARTED WITH MICROSOFT WINDOWS XP

Step 2:   **Choose the Theme and Start Menu**

■ Check with your instructor to see if you are able to modify the desktop and other settings at your school or university. If your network administrator has disabled these commands, skip this step and go to step 3.

■ Point to a blank area on the desktop, click the **right mouse button** to display a context-sensitive menu, then click the **Properties command** to open the Display Properties dialog box. Click the **Themes tab** and select the **Windows XP theme** if it is not already selected. Click **OK**.

■ We prefer to work without any wallpaper (background picture) on the desktop. **Right click** the desktop, click **Properties**, then click the **Desktop tab** in the Display Properties dialog box. Click **None** as shown in Figure 7b, then click **OK**. The background disappears.

■ The Start menu is modified independently of the theme. **Right click** a blank area of the taskbar, click the **Properties command** to display the Taskbar and Start Menu Properties dialog box, then click the **Start Menu tab**.

■ Click the **Start Menu option button**. Click **OK**.

Click Desktop tab

Click right mouse button to display shortcut menu

Click None

Right click blank area on taskbar

(b) Choose the Theme and Start Menu (step 2)

FIGURE 7   Hands-on Exercise 1 (continued)

IMPLEMENT A SCREEN SAVER

A screen saver is a delightful way to personalize your computer and a good way to practice with basic commands in Windows XP. Right click a blank area of the desktop, click the Properties command to open the Display Properties dialog box, then click the Screen Saver tab. Click the down arrow in the Screen Saver list box, choose the desired screen saver, then set the option to wait an appropriate amount of time before the screen saver appears. Click OK to accept the settings and close the dialog box.

New! Larger screen shots with clear callouts.

Boxed tips provide students with additional information.

GETTING STARTED WITH MICROSOFT WINDOWS XP   11

MINI CASES AND PRACTICE EXERCISES

MINI CASES

The Financial Consultant

A friend of yours is in the process of buying a home and has asked you to compare the payments and total interest on a 15- and 30-year loan at varying interest rates. You have decided to analyze the loans in Excel, and then incorporate the results into a memo written in Microsoft Word. As of now, the principal is $150,000, but it is very likely that your friend will change his mind several times, and so you want to use the linking and embedding capability within Windows to dynamically link the worksheet to the word processing document. Your memo should include a letterhead that takes advantage of the formatting capabilities within Word; a graphic logo would be a nice touch.

Fun with the If Statement

Open the *Chapter 4 Mini Case—Fun with the If Statement* workbook in the Exploring Excel folder, then follow the directions in the worksheet to view a hidden message. The message is displayed by various If statements scattered throughout the worksheet, but the worksheet is protected so that you cannot see these formulas. (Use help to see how to protect a worksheet.) We made it easy for you, however, because you can unprotect the worksheet since a password is not required. Once the worksheet is unprotected, pull down the Format menu, click the Cells command, click the Protection tab, and clear the Hidden check box. Prove to your professor that you have done this successfully, by changing the text of our message. Print the completed worksheet to show both displayed values and cell formulas.

The Lottery

Many states raise money through lotteries that advertise prizes of several million dollars. In reality, however, the actual value of the prize is considerably less than the advertised value, although the winners almost certainly do not care. One state, for example, recently offered a twenty million dollar prize that was to be distributed in twenty annual payments of one million dollars each. How much was the prize actually worth, assuming a long-term interest rate of five percent? Use the PV (Present Value) function to determine the answer. What is the effect on the answer if payments to the recipient are made at the beginning of each year, rather than at the end of each year?

A Penny a Day

What if you had a rich un[...]
salary each day for the n[...]
prised at how quickly th[...]
use the Goal Seek comm[...]
(if any) will your uncle pa[...]
uncle pay you on the 31s[...]

The Rule of 72

Delaying your IRA for on[...]
on when you begin. Tha[...]
a calculator, using the "R[...]
long it takes money to [...]
money earning 8% annu[...]
money doubles again in [...]
your IRA at age 21, rath[...]
initial contribution. Use[...]
lose, assuming an 8% ra[...]
determine the exact amo[...]

New!

We've added mini cases at the end of each chapter for expanded practice and review.

New!

Each project in the end-of-chapter material begins at the top of a page—now students can easily see where their assignments begin and end.

PRACTICE WITH EXCEL

1. **Theme Park Admissions:** A partially completed version of the worksheet in Figure 3.13 is available in the Exploring Excel folder as *Chapter 3 Practice 1*. Follow the directions in parts (a) and (b) to compute the totals and format the worksheet, then create each of the charts listed below.

   a. Use the AutoSum command to enter the formulas to compute the total number of admissions for each region and each quarter.

   b. Select the entire worksheet (cells A1 through F8), then use the AutoFormat command to format the worksheet. You do not have to accept the entire design, nor do you have to use the design we selected. You can also modify the design after it has been applied to the worksheet by changing the font size of selected cells and/or changing boldface and italics.

   c. Create a column chart showing the total number of admissions in each quarter as shown in Figure 3.13. Add the graphic shown in the figure for emphasis.

   d. Create a pie chart that shows the percentage of the total number of admissions in each region. Create this chart in its own chart sheet with an appropriate name.

   e. Create a stacked column chart that shows the total number of admissions for each region and the contribution of each quarter within each region. Create this chart in its own chart sheet with an appropriate name.

   f. Create a stacked column chart showing the total number of admissions for each quarter and the contribution of each region within each quarter. Create this chart in its own chart sheet with an appropriate name.

   g. Change the color of each of the worksheet tabs.

   h. Print the entire workbook, consisting of the worksheet in Figure 3.13 plus the three additional sheets that you create. Use portrait orientation for the Sales Data worksheet and landscape orientation for the other worksheets. Create a custom header for each worksheet that includes your name, your course, and your instructor's name. Create a custom footer for each worksheet that includes the name of the worksheet. Submit the completed assignment to your instructor.

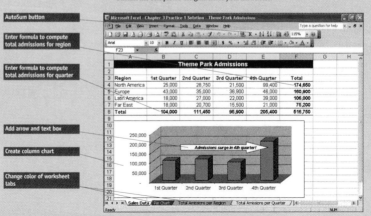

FIGURE 3.13   Theme Park Admissions (exercise 1)

INTEGRATED CASE STUDIES

New!

Each case study contains multiple exercises that use Microsoft Office applications in conjunction with one another.

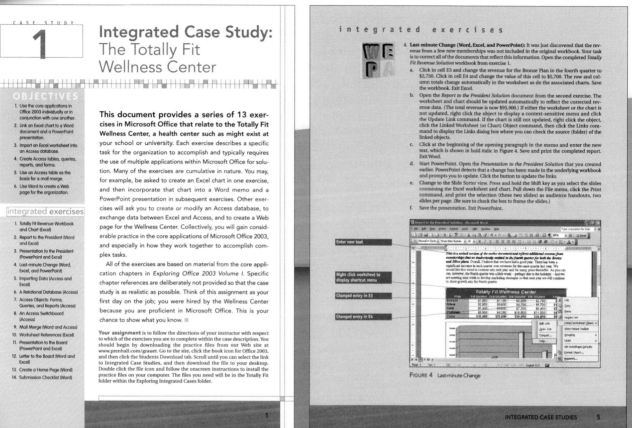

Acknowledgments

We are delighted to have Gretchen Marx as an author on our series. We also want to thank the many individuals who have helped to bring this project to fruition. Jodi McPherson, executive acquisitions editor at Prentice Hall, has provided new leadership in extending the series to Office 2003. Cathi Profitko did an absolutely incredible job on our Web site. Shelly Martin was the creative force behind the chapter-opening case studies. Emily Knight coordinated the marketing and continues to inspire us with suggestions for improving the series. Greg Hubit has been masterful as the external production editor for every book in the series from its inception. Eileen Clark coordinated the myriad details of production and the certification process. Lynne Breitfeller was the project manager and manufacturing buyer. Lori Johnson was the project manager at The GTS Companies and in charge of composition. Chuck Cox did his usual fine work as copyeditor. Melissa Edwards was the supplements editor. Cindy Stevens, Tom McKenzie, and Michael Olmstead wrote the instructor manuals. Michael Fruhbeis developed the innovative and attractive design. We also want to acknowledge our reviewers who, through their comments and constructive criticism, greatly improved the series.

Lynne Band, Middlesex Community College
Don Belle, Central Piedmont Community College
Stuart P. Brian, Holy Family College
Carl M. Briggs, Indiana University School of Business
Kimberly Chambers, Scottsdale Community College
Jill Chapnick, Florida International University
Alok Charturvedi, Purdue University
Jerry Chin, Southwest Missouri State University
Dean Combellick, Scottsdale Community College
Cody Copeland, Johnson County Community College
Larry S. Corman, Fort Lewis College
Janis Cox, Tri-County Technical College
Douglass Cross, Clackamas Community College
Martin Crossland, Southwest Missouri State University
Bill Daley, University of Oregon
Paul E. Daurelle, Western Piedmont Community College
Shawna DePlonty, Sault College of Applied Arts and Technology
Carolyn DiLeo, Westchester Community College
Judy Dolan, Palomar College
David Douglas, University of Arkansas
Carlotta Eaton, Radford University
Judith M. Fitspatrick, Gulf Coast Community College
James Franck, College of St. Scholastica
Raymond Frost, Central Connecticut State University
Susan Fry, Boise State University
Midge Gerber, Southwestern Oklahoma State University
James Gips, Boston College
Vernon Griffin, Austin Community College
Ranette Halverson, Midwestern State University
Michael Hassett, Fort Hays State University
Mike Hearn, Community College of Philadelphia
Wanda D. Heller, Seminole Community College

Bonnie Homan, San Francisco State University
Ernie Ivey, Polk Community College
Walter Johnson, Community College of Philadelphia
Mike Kelly, Community College of Rhode Island
Jane King, Everett Community College
Rose M. Laird, Northern Virginia Community College
David Langley, University of Oregon
John Lesson, University of Central Florida
Maurie Lockley, University of North Carolina at Greensboro
Daniela Marghitu, Auburn University
David B. Meinert, Southwest Missouri State University
Alan Moltz, Naugatuck Valley Technical Community College
Kim Montney, Kellogg Community College
Bill Morse, DeVry Institute of Technology
Kevin Pauli, University of Nebraska
Mary McKenry Percival, University of Miami
Marguerite Nedreberg, Youngstown State University
Jim Pruitt, Central Washington University
Delores Pusins, Hillsborough Community College
Gale E. Rand, College Misericordia
Judith Rice, Santa Fe Community College
David Rinehard, Lansing Community College
Marilyn Salas, Scottsdale Community College
Herach Safarian, College of the Canyons
John Shepherd, Duquesne University
Barbara Sherman, Buffalo State College
Robert Spear, Prince George's Community College
Michael Stewardson, San Jacinto College—North
Helen Stoloff, Hudson Valley Community College
Margaret Thomas, Ohio University
Mike Thomas, Indiana University School of Business
Suzanne Tomlinson, Iowa State University
Karen Tracey, Central Connecticut State University
Antonio Vargas, El Paso Community College
Sally Visci, Lorain County Community College
David Weiner, University of San Francisco
Connie Wells, Georgia State University
Wallace John Whistance-Smith, Ryerson Polytechnic University
Jack Zeller, Kirkwood Community College

A final word of thanks to the unnamed students at the University of Miami who make it all worthwhile. Most of all, thanks to you, our readers, for choosing this book. Please feel free to contact us with any comments and suggestions.

Robert T. Grauer
rgrauer@miami.edu
www.prenhall.com/grauer

Maryann Barber
mbarber@miami.edu

1

Creating a Web Site:
Introduction to Microsoft® Office FrontPage® 2003

OBJECTIVES

After reading this chapter you will be able to:

1. Use FrontPage to create, open, and rename a Web page.

2. Define HTML; explain how to view HTML code within Microsoft FrontPage; modify a Web page by changing its source code.

3. Format text and paragraphs; create a bulleted list; add graphics, horizontal lines, and interactive buttons to a page.

4. Add hyperlinks to a Web page.

5. Create a Web page using FrontPage templates, themes, and layout tables.

6. Add active elements such as an interactive and a marquee to a Web page.

7. View a Web site in Tasks, Navigation, Hyperlinks, and Folders Views; print the Web site structure from Navigation view.

8. Publish the Web site to a floppy disk.

hands-on exercises

1. INTRODUCTION TO HTML
   Input: None
   Output: Web Page

2. TEMPLATES, INTERACTIVE BUTTONS, AND THE PHOTO GALLERY
   Input: Web Page (from exercise 1); File from Prentice Hall Grauer series Web site
   Output: Completed Web Page

3. THE CORPORATE PRESENCE WIZARD
   Input: Web Page (from exercise 2)
   Output: Published Web site

CASE STUDY
THE BETTER SIGNS COMPANY

Janet Olson and Beth Reilly are college roommates with big plans. They have designed a logo for their business school entrepreneurship team and want to make and sell silk-screened T-shirts and other items to raise money to send the team to the national championship competition in June.

They are busy running their fledgling operation, and have recently realized that a Web site could help them publicize their plans and their product to the college community, alumnae, parents, and other supporters of their team. They would like their Web site to include information about them, the rest of the team, and the products that they plan to sell. It will have graphics or pictures of the various items, as well as information on how to contact the team to place an order.

Janet and Beth will develop a complete Web site using the FrontPage Corporate Presence Wizard. They will edit a preset page layout and include pages for each product in the organization's product line, as well as navigation aids to move throughout the Web site. They will apply a theme to the entire Web site so that it has a uniform appearance, and modify some of the default page elements created by the wizard to suit their needs.

In addition to developing the team Web site to publicize their products, Janet and Beth would like to be able to highlight the team's membership. Each person on the team will have their own personal page(s) that can be included in the final design of the site. ■

Your assignment is to read the chapter and complete the hands-on exercises. You will then create your own personal Web page appropriate for publishing on your college or university Web. In addition, you will develop a Web site for your own (fictional) business or organization, modeled after the site you create in the chapter.

You should be creative in your use of themes and/or backgrounds, and should include graphics and a photo gallery of your company's products or services. Your site should include advanced elements such as a marquee and interactive buttons, as well as hyperlinks to both internal and external pages. Finally, you should publish your Web sites to disk so that your instructor can review them.

Sooner or later you are going to want to create a Web page, either to share information about yourself with friends, or to publicize a business or organization to which you belong. Figure 1 displays a home page in *Preview view*, which displays the page as it will appear when viewed in Internet Explorer. It is similar to the one that you will create using Microsoft *FrontPage* in the hands-on exercises that follow (the toolbars have been removed to show more of the page). The page in Figure 1 contains several elements that you will add as you create and modify Janet Olson's home page. *Bulleted* (and *numbered*) *lists* are used to organize *hyperlinks*, which in turn are used to link your home page to other pages you develop, or to other pages on the Web. *Horizontal lines* are used to break up parts of the page to help organize the text and topics on the page.

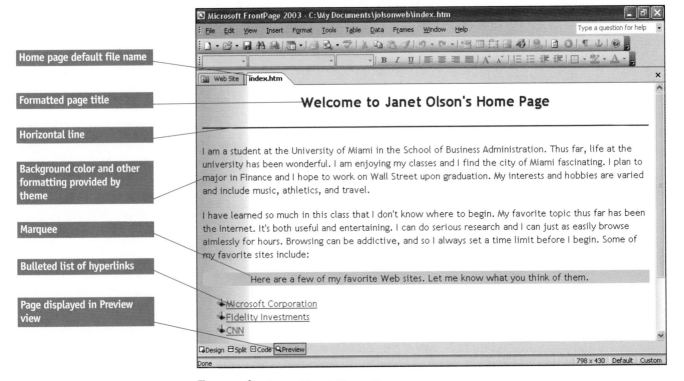

Home page default file name

Formatted page title

Horizontal line

Background color and other formatting provided by theme

Marquee

Bulleted list of hyperlinks

Page displayed in Preview view

FIGURE 1   Janet Olson's Home Page

The *marquee*, the aqua text bar that extends across the middle of the page, contains text that you want to be sure your visitor reads. In the actual Web page the text scrolls continuously across the screen from right to left. You can modify the color of the marquee and/or the color of the text, change the delay time before the marquee appears, and provide other formatting as you choose. The home page background coloration is provided by a theme in FrontPage. A *theme* adds formatting elements to a Web page and creates coordinated background, text, and hyperlink colors for a pleasing design.

In order to have other people visit your Web page you have to publish it to a *Web server*, a special purpose computer that is connected to the Internet and that presents to online visitors the Web pages it stores. While you will not actually send to a Web server the pages that you create, they will have the look and feel of Web pages you see when you access the World Wide Web.

Hypertext Markup Language (HTML)

In the early days of the Web, you had to use *Hypertext Markup Language (HTML)* to create a Web page. HTML consists of a set of codes (also known as *HTML tags*) that describe how the document is to appear when viewed in a Web browser such as Internet Explorer. Each of these codes was entered explicitly in a text editor such as Notepad. Developing a Web page today is much easier, as an *HTML editor* such as *Microsoft FrontPage* generates the codes for you. You enter the text of a document in FrontPage *Design view*, apply basic formatting such as boldface or italics, and add graphics or other elements as appropriate. FrontPage does the rest and automatically saves the file as an HTML document suitable for display on the Web and/or viewing with a Web browser.

Figure 2 is in *Code view* and shows the underlying HTML tags that format the page in Figure 1. The tags are enclosed in angle brackets and generally occur in pairs at the beginning and end of the text to be formatted, with the ending code preceded by a slash. In Figure 2, for example, the text "Janet Olson's Home Page" is enclosed within the *<title> </title>* tags. The function of the *title tag* is to indicate what will be displayed in the Internet Explorer title bar when the page is viewed in the browser's application window. Look at the title and other tags in Figure 2, then observe the effect of these tags as they are read and displayed in Preview view in Figure 1.

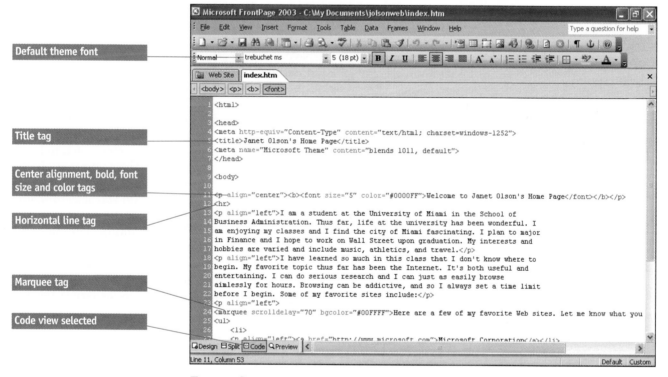

FIGURE 2 HTML Code

Tags can be nested within one another. The welcome message in the page header in Figure 2 is nested within codes to center (*<align="center">*) and boldface (*<strong>*) the text, as well as tags to display it in a different color and larger font size (*<font color="#0000FF" size="5">*). The ***anchor tag*** (*<a></a>*), which is not visible in the figure, allows you to create a hyperlink to jump to another page on the Web or document in the current Web site. You use the *href* (for hyperlink reference) parameter and enclose the Internet address within the anchor tags. Note, too, that some tags appear individually rather than in pairs, such as the <hr> tag that indicates a horizontal rule or line.

FrontPage Toolbars

Figure 3 displays the FrontPage screen used to create a new Web page. It shows the FrontPage editing window in Design view, where you will create most, if not all of your pages. It also shows the open *task pane* at the right of the window where you can open an existing page or get help from Microsoft Office Online. (The task pane changes depending on what feature in FrontPage you are using.)

Look carefully and you will see that the toolbars are subtly different from those in other Microsoft Office applications. The Standard toolbar, for example, includes the Insert Hyperlink button, as well as additional tools such as the Insert Picture and Web Component buttons. It also contains a button to preview the page in Internet Explorer.

The Formatting toolbar contains tools to increase and decrease font size, as well as a drop-down list box to specify a specific point size. The Formatting toolbar in Figure 3 also has tools to create bulleted and numbered lists, and to highlight text or change the text color.

Hyperlinks and Themes

One of the things that makes the Web so useful is the ability to jump from one page to the next. It doesn't matter if the linked documents are on the same server (computer) or if they are on an entirely different computer. Either way, you can go from one document to another simply by clicking on the links of interest to you. It's apparent, therefore, that if you are to develop a meaningful home page, you must learn how to include hyperlinks of your own.

Figure 4 shows the same page as Figure 1, but using a different theme. The visible hyperlinks appear as underlined text; click on a desired link and Internet Explorer (or other browser) displays the associated document. A lilac link indicates that the associated page has not been previously displayed; deep red on the other hand, indicates that the page has already been viewed at least once. (These colors change, depending on the theme in use for that page.)

To create an external link to a page on the Internet, you either need to know the Internet address of the associated page or have recently visited the page. In the latter instance, FrontPage 2003 will find the list of recently visited sites in the Internet Explorer History list (or stored by your default browser), and you select the link from the list as shown in the figure. If the link is to a local document on your PC rather than to an external Web page you will select the appropriate file. This enables you to link one document, such as your home page, to a second document that might describe your hobbies and interests, which in turn can be linked to additional documents. Whether linking to Web sites or internal documents, you need not concern yourself with the syntax of the HTML tags, as FrontPage will prompt you for the necessary information.

LEARNING BY DOING

By now, you are undoubtedly an experienced Web surfer and have an extensive list of favorite Web sites. Typically, you start at a Web address such as **www.microsoft.com**, and click hyperlinks to jump to other pages within that site, or to other sites on the Internet. If you think of all the Web pages of an organization as a hierarchy, the *home page* is the uppermost page in an organization's Web site. A *Web site* is the collection of all the pages accessible from the home page. In this chapter you will first develop a personal Web site and home page for Janet Olson, the fictional student introduced at the beginning of the chapter. Then you will create a complete Web site for the fictional student organization that Janet belongs to, T-shirts To Go, and publish her personal page to it. You will create your own site in one of the end-of-chapter exercises.

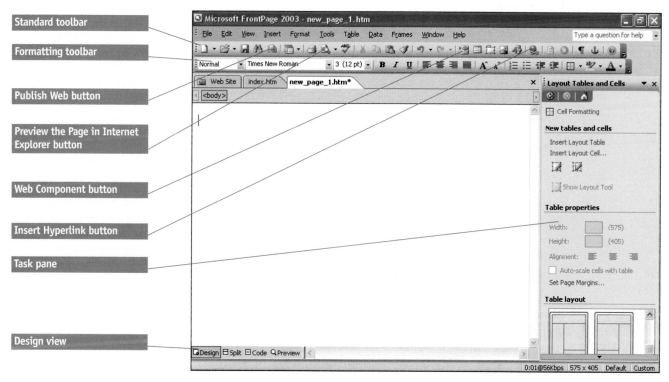

Labels (left to right / top to bottom):
- Standard toolbar
- Formatting toolbar
- Publish Web button
- Preview the Page in Internet Explorer button
- Web Component button
- Insert Hyperlink button
- Task pane
- Design view

FIGURE 3 FrontPage Toolbars

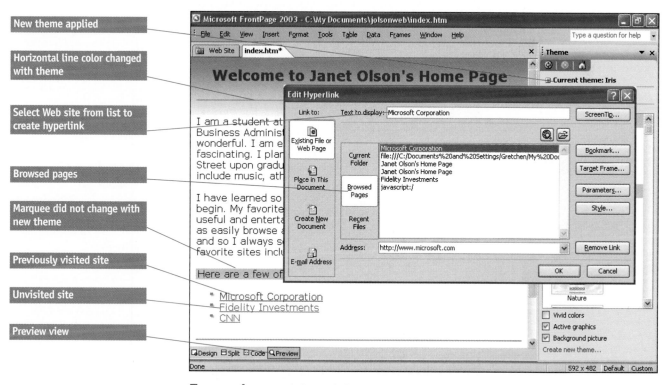

Labels:
- New theme applied
- Horizontal line color changed with theme
- Select Web site from list to create hyperlink
- Browsed pages
- Marquee did not change with new theme
- Previously visited site
- Unvisited site
- Preview view

FIGURE 4 Hyperlinks and Themes

1 Introduction to HTML

Objective To use FrontPage to create a simple home page, insert a marquee, and use formatting commands. Use Figure 5 as a guide in the exercise.

Step 1: Create a Personal Web Site

- Click the **Start button**, select **Programs**, select **Microsoft Office**, then click **FrontPage**. (If you do not see FrontPage on the Start menu, request assistance from your instructor or campus help desk.)

- If you do not see the FrontPage toolbars, pull down the **View menu**, click **Toolbars** then click **Standard**. Right click the **Standard toolbar** and select **Formatting** from the shortcut menu. If a new blank page is displayed with a page tab of new_page_1.htm, click the **Close button** in the upper right corner of the page.

- Pull down the **File menu** and select **New** to display the New task pane in Figure 5a. In the list under **New Web site** click **One page Web site** to display the Web Site Templates dialog box in the figure.

- Click in the text box to **Specify the location of the new Web site**. Enter **c:\My Documents\jolsonweb**, or the location given to you by your instructor. (If you are in a computer lab or working on a shared computer, ask for help from your campus help desk on how to specify the network location where you will save your work.)

- Click **OK** to close the dialog box and create the Web site.

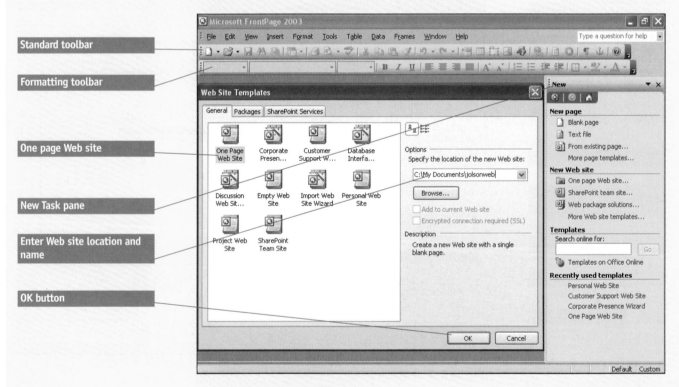

(a) Create a Personal Web Site (step 1)

FIGURE 5 Hands-on Exercise 1

Step 2: Create a Bulleted List

- The new personal Web site is displayed in Folders view (note that the Folders button at the bottom of the window is highlighted). Double click **index.htm**, Janet Olson's home page, to open it in Design view.

- Type the text for Janet Olson's home page title as shown in Figure 5b, then select the text. Click the **down arrow** next to the Font Size box and select size 5 (18 pt) to enlarge the title for your page, then click the **Center** and **Bold buttons**.

- Press **Enter** to move to a new line. Click the **Align Left button**, then click **Bold** on the Formatting toolbar to change the formatting. Click the **down arrow** next to the Font Size box and select size **3 (12 pt)**. Enter the rest of the text as shown in Figure 5b.

- Enter the text for the hyperlinks, **Microsoft Corporation**, **Fidelity Investments**, and **CNN**. (FrontPage will automatically double-space the text.)

- Click and drag to select the three links, then click the **Bullets button** on the Formatting toolbar. Each link is single-spaced and preceded by a bullet, as shown in Figure 5b.

- Pull down the **File menu**, then click the **Save command** (or click the **Save button** on the Standard toolbar).

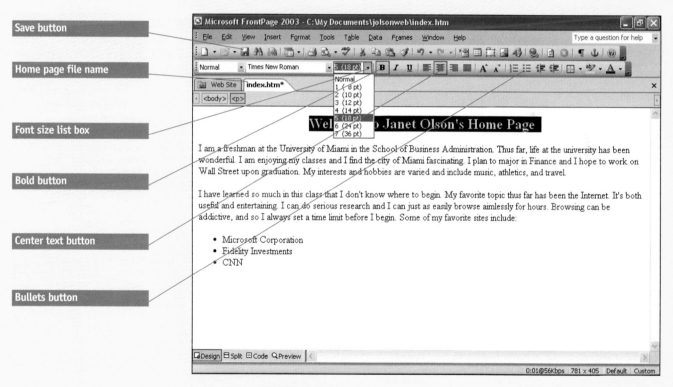

(b) Create a Bulleted List (step 2)

FIGURE 5 Hands-on Exercise 1 *(continued)*

SELECT-THEN-DO

All formatting operations in FrontPage use the select-then-do approach; that is, you select a block of text, then you execute the command to operate on that text. You can select the text in different ways, the most basic of which is to click and drag over the desired characters. You can also use standard MS Office shortcuts, such as double click to select a word and press Shift+End to select to the end of the current line.

Step 3: Create and Test the Hyperlinks

- Click and drag to select the phrase **Microsoft Corporation**. Pull down the **Insert menu** and click **Hyperlink** to display the Insert Hyperlink dialog box in Figure 5c.

- Click in the **Address text box**, then enter the Web address of the site you want to link to, **www.microsoft.com** (FrontPage automatically inserts http:// in front of the address). Click **OK** to close the Insert Hyperlink dialog box and create the hyperlink.

- Insert the additional hyperlinks to the Web addresses **http://www.fidelity.com** and **http://www.cnn.com**, respectively. Click the **Save button** on the Standard toolbar.

- Click the **Preview button** at the bottom of the window to change to preview mode.

- Click the **Microsoft** hyperlink. You should see the Microsoft home page in Preview mode. If you are unable to connect, click the **Design button** to return to design view. Right click the hyperlink, then select **Hyperlink Properties**. Correct the invalid link, then test it again in Preview mode.

- Test the various other links to be sure that they are working. Make any necessary corrections, then click the **Design button** to return to design view.

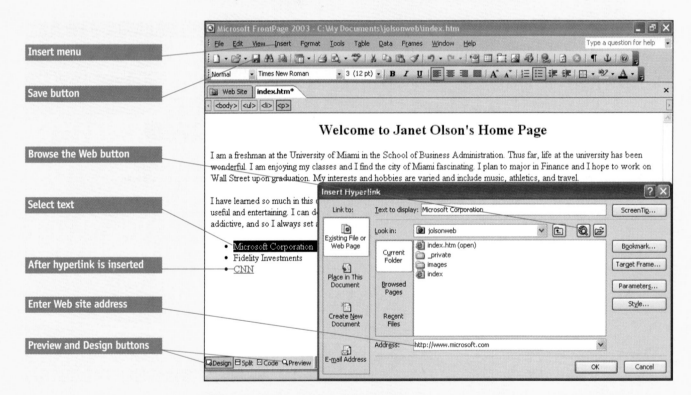

(c) Create and Test the Hyperlinks (step 3)

FIGURE 5 Hands-on Exercise 1 (*continued*)

BROWSE TO THE PAGE

You don't have to remember the URL in order to create a hyperlink. Click the Browse the Web button in the Insert Hyperlink dialog box and navigate in your browser to the page for which you want to create the hyperlink. When the page is displayed in your browser, press Alt+Tab to return to FrontPage. The Internet address is automatically entered in the Insert Hyperlink dialog box.

Step 4: Format the Page

- Click and drag to select the page heading at the top of Janet Olson's Web page (or click in the white space to the left of the title to select the whole line). Pull down the **Format menu**, then click **Font** to display the Font dialog box shown in Figure 5d.

- Click the **drop-down arrow** on the Background color list box, then click **Blue** to change the color of the selected text. Click **OK** to close the dialog box.

- Click in front of "I am a freshman…" to position the insertion point at the beginning of the first paragraph. Pull down the **Insert menu** and select **Horizontal Line** to insert a horizontal rule above the paragraph.

- Position the insertion point at the end of the last hyperlink and press **Enter** twice. Insert another horizontal line.

- Save the document.

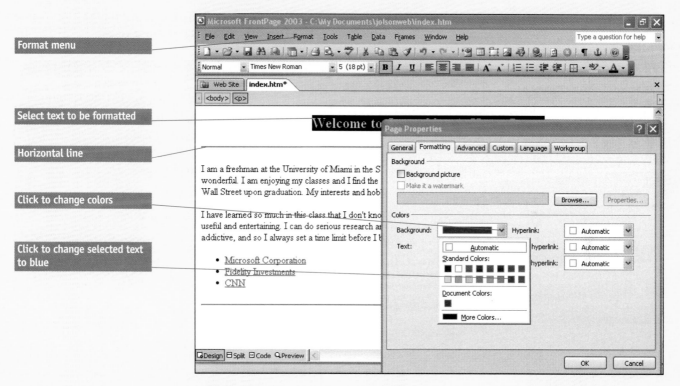

(d) Format the Page (step 4)

FIGURE 5 Hands-on Exercise 1 (*continued*)

USE GOOD DESIGN

The principles of good graphic design apply to home pages as well as to newsletters and other written work. Limit yourself to two or three fonts and/or font sizes. Use boldface, italics, and underline sparingly or else the effect is lost. And finally, don't overload a page with graphics or else the user is apt to lose interest as he or she waits for the page to be displayed over a modem.

Step 5: Insert a Marquee

- Click at the end of the second paragraph immediately after the colon following the word "include." Press **Enter** to insert a blank line.

- Pull down the **Insert menu**, select **Web Component** (or click the **Web Component button** on the Standard toolbar) to display the Insert Web Component dialog box. Dynamic Effects is chosen by default in the Component type list. Select **Marquee** from the Choose an effect list at the right of the dialog box, then click **Finish** to display the Marquee Properties dialog box in Figure 5e.

- Enter the text shown in the figure. Change the Speed Delay to **70** (to speed up the marquee's first appearance on the page). Click the **drop-down arrow** on the Background Color list box, and select a background color.

- Be sure the text box next to **Repeat Continuously** (not visible in the figure) is checked. Click **OK**. The marquee is inserted on the page. Save the page.

- Click the **Preview button** at the bottom of the page to view the marquee scrolling across the page. Click **Design** to return to design view.

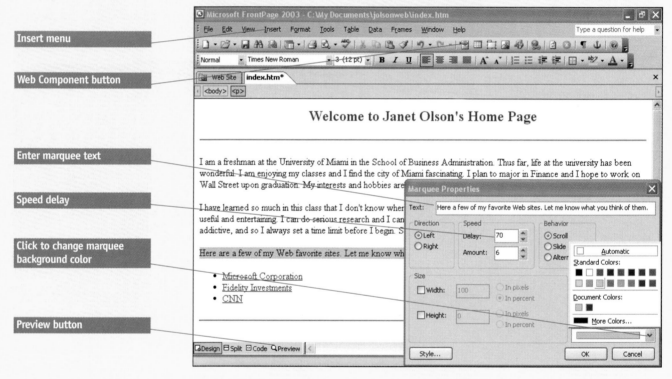

(e) Insert a Marquee (step 5)

FIGURE 5   Hands-on Exercise 1 (*continued*)

CONTINUOUS MARQUEES

Marquees scroll continuously across the page. If your marquee is only a few words long, you'll end up with a lot of blank space between the end of one marquee display and the beginning of the next. Try typing your message two or three times back-to-back in the Marquee Properties dialog box, then see which one looks best when viewed in Internet Explorer.

Step 6: **Change the Background Color**

- Pull down the **Format menu** and click **Background** to display the Page Properties dialog box in Figure 5f. (If you don't see the Background option in the Format menu, click the double arrow at the bottom of the menu to display additional choices.) If necessary, click the **Formatting tab**.

- Click the **drop-down arrow** in the Background colors list box to display the color choices. You could select a standard color. Instead, click **More Colors** to display the color prism in Figure 5f. Select a color (we chose lavender), then click **OK** to close the More Colors dialog box.

- Click **OK** to close the Page Properties dialog box. The home page displays the new background color. Save the document.

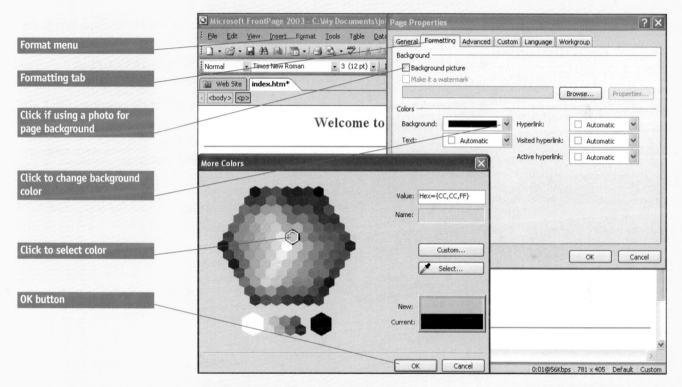

(f) Change the Background Color (step 6)

FIGURE 5 Hands-on Exercise 1 (*continued*)

USE A PICTURE FOR THE BACKGROUND

FrontPage allows you to use a photo as a background for your Web page. Pull down the Format menu and click Background, then click the Background Picture check box. Click the Browse button to navigate to the folder where you have stored the photo that you want to use as a background image. Select the image file, then click Open to select the file and close the dialog box. Click OK to close the Page Properties dialog box. As always, if you don't like the effect you can click the Undo button or press Ctrl+Z to undo the effects of the change.

Step 7: View the HTML Code

- Click the **Split button** to display the HTML source code together with your page as shown in Figure 5g. FrontPage has created all of the necessary HTML tags for you.

- Scroll up in the code window and position the insertion point to the left of the closing **</head>** tag (below the last meta tag, which should be around line 5). Press **Enter** to insert a blank line.

- Enter < (the key combination is **Shift+,**). The drop-down list of HTML tags in the figure is displayed. Type the letter **t** to select the title tag, then press **Enter** to insert the tag in the document. Enter > (the key combination is **Shift+.**). The beginning and ending title tags are inserted in the document with the insertion point between them.

- Enter **Janet Olson's Home Page**. This action changes the title displayed in the title bar when you open the page in Internet Explorer.

- Select the letters after the bgcolor tag (background color) **CCCCFF** and change them to **FFFFCC**. Be sure that you do this without deleting the pound sign (#).

- Change the word **freshman** to **student** within the code window. Click the Preview button to see the effects of the changes.

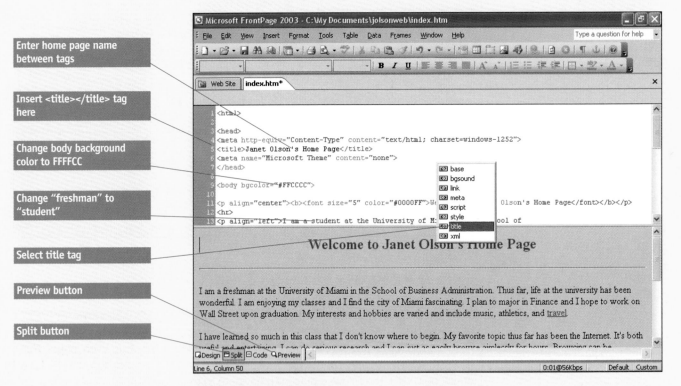

(g) View the HTML Code (step 7)

FIGURE 5   Hands-on Exercise 1 (*continued*)

THE HTML BACKGROUND COLOR TAG

The HTML tag that specifies the background color of lavender for our home page is <body bgcolor="#CCCCFF">. A different combination of symbols yields a different color. #FFFF00, for example, produces a yellow background. Go to the Web site http://users.rcn.com/giant.interport/COLOR/1ColorSpecifier.html to see other color codes.

Step 8: Add a Theme

- Click the **Design button** at the bottom of the window to return to the page editing view. Pull down the **Format menu** and click **Theme**. (If the Theme command is not visible, click the double arrow at the bottom of the menu to show additional options.)

- The Theme task pane in Figure 5h is displayed. (We hid the toolbars to display more of the task pane.)

- Scroll down in the Select a Theme box and click various themes to preview them in your Web page at the left of the window. (If you see a warning message the cascading style sheets and/or author-time web components are not activated, follow the instructions to activate the missing feature.)

- Click the down arrow next to theme you want to apply (we chose **Blends**) and click **Apply as default theme**. This will ensure that all new pages in Janet's Web will contain the same theme, an important principle in Web design. The background color you selected in Step 7 changes to the default color in the theme. Other elements that you already formatted, such as the color of the marquee, are not changed.

- Click the **Save button** on the Standard toolbar to save your page.

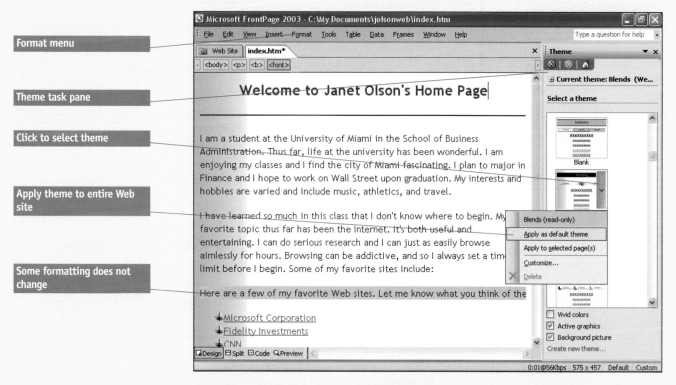

(h) Add a Theme (step 8)

FIGURE 5 Hands-on Exercise 1 (*continued*)

CUSTOMIZE A THEME

Themes are great, but you may not find one that suits your purpose. You can customize a theme's color, bullet style, and so on by clicking the down arrow next to the theme in the Theme task pane, then clicking Customize to display the Customize Theme dialog box. Click Colors, Graphics, and/or Text to customize every/any aspect of the theme, then save it with its own name so that you can use your theme again.

Step 9:   **View the Page in Internet Explorer**

- Click the **Preview button** to view your home page as it will appear in Internet Explorer. The entry in the title bar has not changed, but the text and formatting of the document has, corresponding to the changes you made in previous steps. Click **Design button** to return to Design view.

- Pull down the **File** menu and select **Preview in browser**. When FrontPage displays a message asking you to choose the screen resolution, choose whichever resolution you want. The page is displayed in Internet Explorer as shown in Figure 5i.
  - ❏ Note the page title in the Internet Explorer title bar. It should say Janet Olson's Home Page as this is the page title you entered in Code view in Step 7.

- Click the **FrontPage button** on the Windows taskbar to return to FrontPage. Preview the page in another screen resolution.

- Close Internet Explorer, then close FrontPage if you do not wish to continue at this time.

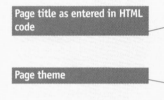

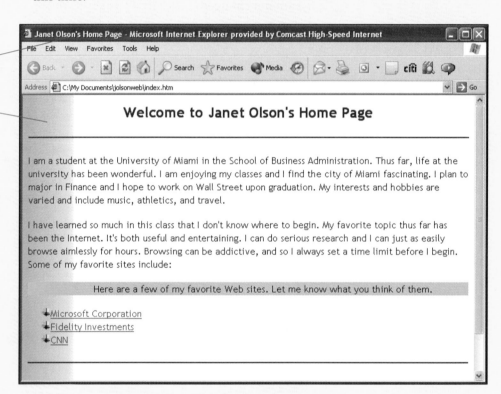

(i) View the Page in Internet Explorer (step 9)

FIGURE 5   Hands-on Exercise 1 (*continued*)

THE FILE NAME VERSUS THE PAGE TITLE

The file name index.htm is the name by which Windows stores and organizes the home page on disk. The file name is used in the Internet address, such as www.anyu.edu/students/jolsonweb/index.htm to create a hyperlink to the file. The page title (between the <title> tags in HTML view) on the other hand, is the way the page will be indexed by a search engine database, hence is very important. The page title should be as descriptive and representative as possible, so that it will show up in a key word search using a search engine such as Google.

FRONTPAGE TEMPLATES

FrontPage includes a number of page templates that you can use in designing your Web pages. A ***template*** simplifies the creation of a page, because the margins of any tables used within the template are automatically set up by FrontPage. Figure 6 shows the Header, Body, Footer, and Left template as it appears when you open it in FrontPage. The Layout Tables and Cells task pane at the right of the window allows you to select the desired template, insert new cells, and change other table and page properties.

The page is essentially created using a multi-columned table called a ***layout table***, which you then fill with your own headings and text. The numbers that appear in drop-down boxes on the edges of the table indicate the number of pixels in that segment of the line that creates the edge of the table or table cell. A ***pixel*** is one of the programmable picture elements that make up your screen display. Thus, FrontPage allows you to change the size of the cell down to the pixel level, giving the developer complete control over the layout of the page.

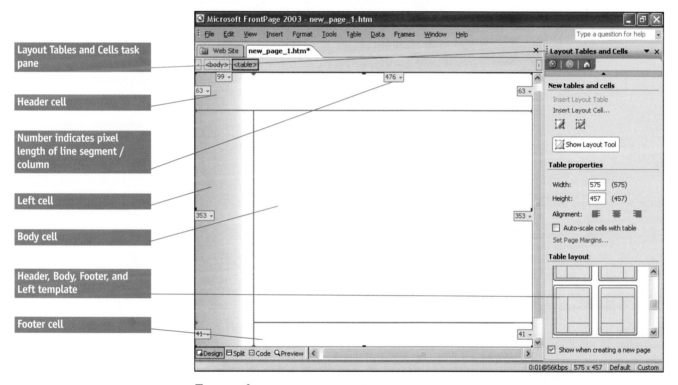

Layout Tables and Cells task pane

Header cell

Number indicates pixel length of line segment / column

Left cell

Body cell

Header, Body, Footer, and Left template

Footer cell

FIGURE 6 A FrontPage Template

AUTOSTRETCH

When you select a page layout from the task pane, FrontPage uses cell sizes that fit the visible area of the page, not including that taken up by the task pane itself or any toolbars you have visible. If you want your layout to stretch to take up the entire page no matter what screen size or resolution the page visitor is using, you will need to make the column/row you are working on automatically stretch to fill the screen. To do this, click the edge of the cell you are working on, then click the down arrow next to the size indicator and select Make Column Autostretch. Since your site visitors may have different screen resolutions, Autostretch will also ensure that the page shrinks to fit the available size of someone viewing your page at a lower resolution than you used when designing it.

The Web was designed with graphic files in mind, and it is a fantastic medium for sharing drawings, pictures, photos, and other graphics. FrontPage 2003 allows you to create a photo gallery in a Web page. A *photo gallery* is a layout in which you display photos (or other digitized artwork) that you have scanned or downloaded from the Web or a digital camera. You select the layout, then insert a thumbnail image of each photo into the gallery. A *thumbnail* is a compressed version of the original photo that is a much smaller file size and therefore keeps the page from downloading too slowly. You can edit the pictures within the photo gallery to change their size, rotate, and/or crop each image. You can also add captions as shown in the figure. When you save the Web page, FrontPage prompts you to save the embedded photos with the page so that when the visitor clicks the thumbnail image, the entire photo is displayed.

Figure 7 shows the template page as it will look after you have completed the next hands-on exercise. The body cell contains the photo gallery about Janet's London trip, complete with images and text from each locale she visited. The header cell was used for the page title. The cell at the left of the window contains an *interactive button* to navigate back to Janet's home page. It could also contain buttons to link to other pages in Jane's Web once she creates them. The footer cell contains a time stamp and e-mail link so that the viewer can contact Janet. A *time stamp* indicates when the page was last updated and gives the viewer some indication of how current the information is.

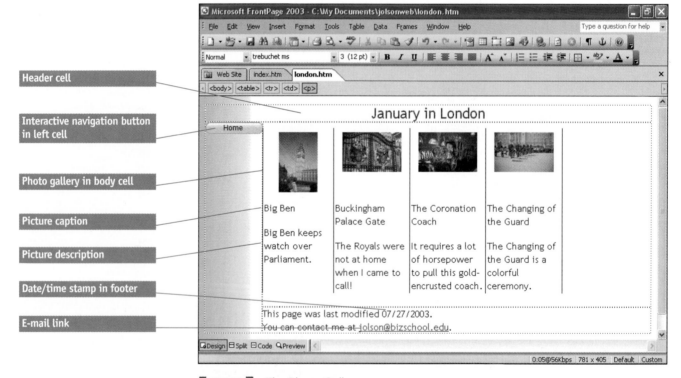

FIGURE 7 The Photo Gallery

PUBLISHING YOUR PHOTOS TO THE WEB

Many Web portals such as Yahoo, Excite, AOL, and others, allow you to create your own personal Web site (usually with a limited amount of storage). Create a home page with a link to your photo gallery, and you can share your vacation, new car, or addition to the family in a matter of minutes.

Templates, Interactive Buttons, and the Photo Gallery

Objective To create a Web page using a FrontPage template; to add a photo gallery and interactive button. Use Figure 8 as a guide in the exercise.

Step 1: **Open a Template**

- Start FrontPage as you normally do. If FrontPage opens a site other than Janet Olson's Web site from the first hands-on exercise, pull down the **File menu**, then select **Close Site**.

- If Janet Olson's Web site is not open, pull down the **File menu**, then select **Open Site**. Click the down arrow next to the **Look in textbox** and navigate to the folder containing Janet Olson's Web site.) Click **Open** to open the site, then double click the file **index.htm** to open the home page.

- Click the **Create a new normal page button** on the Standard toolbar to open a new blank page. If necessary, click the down arrow at the top of the task pane and select **Layout Tables and Cells** to match the screen in Figure 8a. (If the task pane is not displayed at the right of the window, pull down the **View menu**, select **Task pane**, then follow the instructions above to display the layout table options.)

- Scroll down in the **Layout Table list box** and click the **Header, Body, Footer, and Left** layout as shown in the figure.

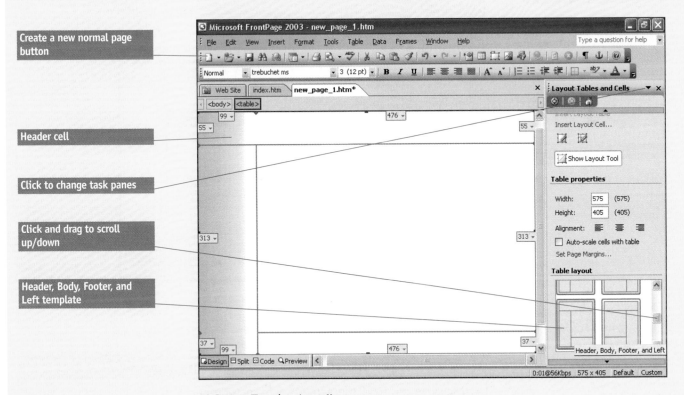

Create a new normal page button

Header cell

Click to change task panes

Click and drag to scroll up/down

Header, Body, Footer, and Left template

(a) Open a Template (step 1)

FIGURE 8 Hands-on Exercise 2

Step 2: Modify the Template

- If you do not see the table border, pull down the **Table menu**, click **Select**, then select **Layout Table**. Click the down arrow next to the number at the top left edge of the layout table and select **Make Column Autostretch** as shown in Figure 8b (the page heading is not yet entered), to ensure that the page will expand/shrink to fit any screen size and resolution.

- Click in the header cell and enter **January in London**. Click the **Center button** on the Standard toolbar to center the page heading. Select the heading text, then change the font size to **5 (18 pt)** and the color to **blue** as you did in the first hands-on exercise.

- Click the **Save button** on the Standard toolbar. Click the **Change Title button** in the Save As dialog box and enter **January in London** as the page title, which will display in Internet Explorer title bar when the page is opened.

- Click **OK** to close the Set Page Title dialog box, then enter the name **london** in the File name text box. Click **Save** to save the page and close the Save As dialog box.

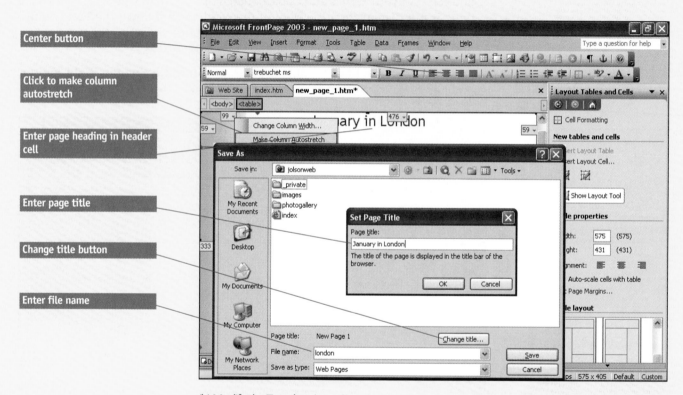

(b) Modify the Template (step 2)

FIGURE 8   Hands-on Exercise 2 (*continued*)

USING LAYOUT TABLES IN A WEB PAGE

HTML does not have the same text formatting capabilities as a word processor such as Microsoft Word. You will look in vain for a ruler bar, tab settings, and Insert Column button in Design view. Page layout is accomplished through tables, and is greatly simplified by the use of templates for one-, two-, and three column layouts.

Step 3: Download the Photos

- Open Internet Explorer and enter **www.prenhall.com/grauer** in the **Address text box**. Click the **Office 2003 series text cover** to jump to the Exploring Microsoft Office 2003 series Web site.

- Click the **Student Downloads tab** at the top of the page, then scroll down in the resulting page to the Application Modules section shown in Figure 8c. (If you have trouble with this method, you can try entering the address of the Office 2003 series, http://wps.prenhall.com/bp_grauer_exploring2003_1, directly in the address bar.)

- Click the download link in the Student Data Disks column next to **Exploring Microsoft FrontPage 2003** to display the File Download dialog box in the figure, then click **Open** to begin the download process.

- You will see a dialog box indicating that the file download process has begun, then a message from Bob Grauer and Maryann Barber, the series authors, is displayed. Click **OK** to close the WinZip self-extractor message from Bob and Maryann and display the WinZip Self-Extractor dialog box.

- Click **Unzip** to extract the photo files to the default directory on the c: drive. Click **OK** to close the message that indicates the files have been unzipped, then click **Close** to close the self-extractor. Close Internet Explorer and return to FrontPage.

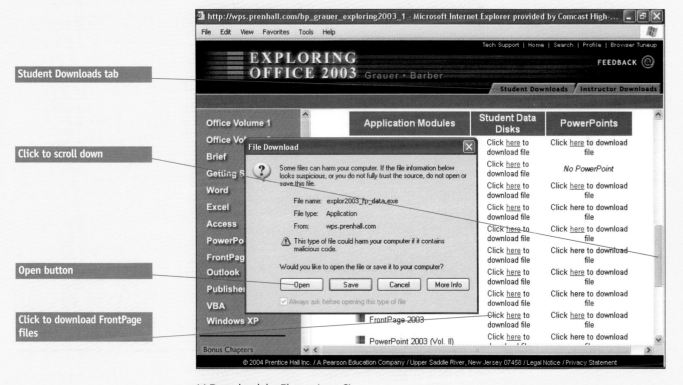

(c) Download the Photos (step 3)

FIGURE 8   Hands-on Exercise 2 (*continued*)

INSERTING MULTIMEDIA FILES

You can insert multimedia files in any Web page you design. However, multimedia objects take time to download, so it is better to include a link to these objects in your page. If visitors want to open the file, they click the link; others can ignore the link and avoid the wait.

Step 4: **Create the Photo Gallery**

- Click the **london.htm tab** to display the page. Close the Task pane. Click in the empty body cell below the page heading, pull down the **Insert menu** and select **Picture**, then click **New Photo Gallery** to display the dialog box in Figure 8d.

- Click the **Layout tab** in the dialog box, then click **Horizontal Layout**. Click in the **Number of pictures per row drop down list** and change it to **4**.

- Click the **Pictures tab**, click the **Add button**, then select **Pictures from Files** to display the File Open dialog box. Click the down arrow next to the **Look in text box** and navigate to **C:\Exploring FrontPage** (or select the folder where you extracted the photos in Step 3).

- Select **Big Ben.jpg**, then click **Open** to insert the image and close the dialog box. Enter a caption for the photo in the **Caption text box** (we entered Big Ben), then enter text in the **Description text box** as shown in the figure.

- Click the **Add button** again and follow the same procedure to add **BuckGate.jpg**, **Coach.jpg**, and **TheGuard.jpg** to the photo gallery. Enter a caption and description for each photo, using Figure 6 as a guide. Click **OK** to close the dialog box and return to the page.

- Click the **Save button** on the Standard toolbar, then, when the Save Embedded Files dialog box is displayed, click **OK** to save the photos with the Web page.

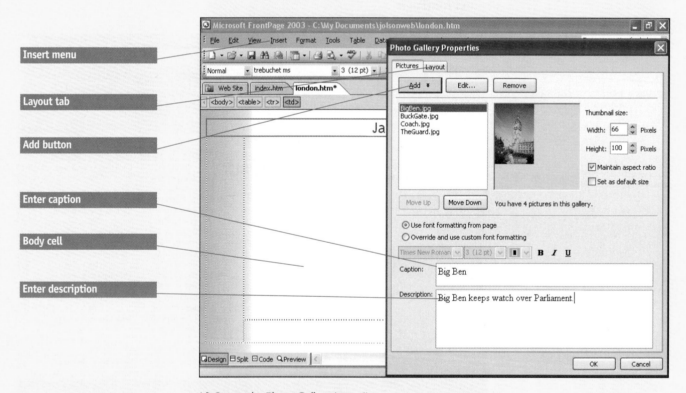

(d) Create the Photo Gallery (step 4)

FIGURE 8 Hands-on Exercise 2 (*continued*)

THUMBNAILS

To keep download time to a minimum, the FrontPage Photo Gallery automatically creates thumbnails of your photos. Even so, a large photo gallery will take a long time to download for someone using a 56kB modem. If you have a lot of photos to display, try creating multiple photo gallery pages and then creating links from one page to another.

Step 5: Insert an Interactive Button

- Click in the empty cell at the left of the page. Pull down the **Insert menu**, then select **Web Component** (or click the **Web Component button** on the Standard toolbar) to display the Insert Web Component dialog box.

- Click the **Interactive Button** in the Choose an effect list box, then click **Finish** to display the Interactive Buttons dialog box (partially obscured) in Figure 8e. Scroll down in the **Buttons list box** and click the various buttons to preview them. Select a button that coordinates with your theme (we chose **Metal Capsule 4**).

- Enter **Home** in the **Text text box**. Click the **Browse button** next to the Link text box to display the Edit Hyperlink dialog box shown in the figure.

- Select **index.htm**, then click **OK** to close the Edit Hyperlink dialog box. Click **OK** to close the Interactive Buttons dialog box and insert the button in your page. It is located halfway down the cell instead of at the top, and the theme is not showing through properly.

- Right click the **Home button** that you just inserted and select **Button properties** from the shortcut menu to display the Interactive Buttons dialog box. Click the **Image tab**, then click the **Make the button a GIF image and use a transparent background option button**. Click **OK** to close the dialog box.

- Click the button, then pull town the **Table menu** and select **Table Properties**, then click **Cell**. In the Cell Properties dialog box, click the down arrow in the Vertical alignment drop-down box and select **Top**. Click **OK** to close the dialog box.

- Click the **Save button** on the Standard toolbar, then when the Save Embedded Files dialog box displays, click **OK** to save the button with the page.

- Press **Ctrl+Click** to follow the hyperlink. You should jump to Janet's home page.

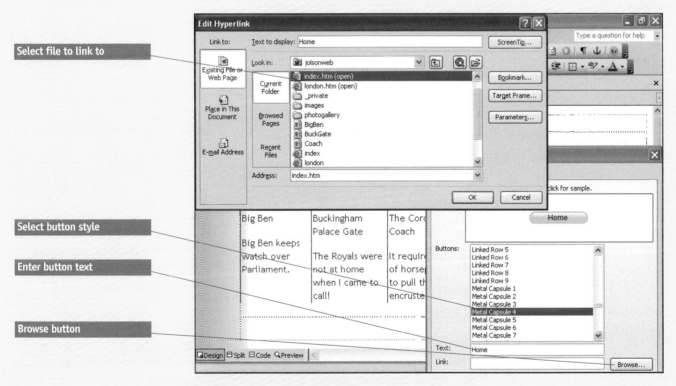

(e) Insert an Interactive Button (step 5)

FIGURE 8   Hands-on Exercise 2 (*continued*)

Step 6: Check the Hyperlinks

- Pull down the **View menu** and click **Folder List** to display the folders and files in the current Web site. Pull down the **View menu** once again and select **Hyperlinks** to change to hyperlinks view.

- If you do not see the hyperlinks shown in Figure 8f, double click the file **index.htm** in the folder list.
    - ❏ Note that while there is a hyperlink from the January in London page to Janet's home page, there is no way to get from the home page to January in London.

- Double click **index.htm** in the hyperlinks diagram to open the home page in design view. Double click the word **travel** at the end of the first paragraph of text to select it, then right click the word and select **Hyperlink** from the short-cut menu to display the Insert Hyperlink dialog box.

- If necessary, click **Current Folder**, then select **london.htm**. The Address text box should display the file name. Click **OK** to insert the hyperlink. The word travel now appears as a hyperlink.

- Press **Ctrl+Click** to test the hyperlink. You should jump to the January in London page. Click the **index.htm tab** to return to the home page, then save the page. Pull down the **File menu** and click **Close Site**. Close FrontPage if you do not want to continue.

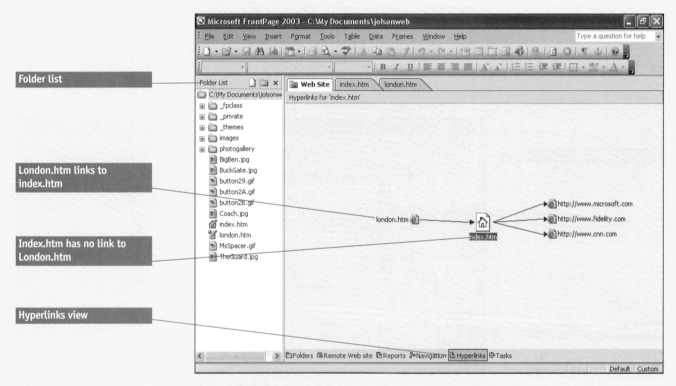

Folder list

London.htm links to index.htm

Index.htm has no link to London.htm

Hyperlinks view

(f) Check the Hyperlinks (step 6)

FIGURE 8 Hands-on Exercise 2 (*continued*)

THE INTRANET

Web pages placed on a local area network (LAN) for use exclusively within the organization are known as an intranet. They can be used to publish employee handbooks, training and operations manuals, and other internal documents.

As defined by FrontPage 2003 a *Web site* is more than a collection of related Web pages. When you create a site, FrontPage generates and stores internal indices, links, and other data that it uses to track the various pages in the site and the relationships between them. In order to save all of this internal data, you must *publish* your Web site to a Web server instead of merely copying it.

Creating a FrontPage Web site allows you to apply a theme to the entire site. It allows you to create standard text that appears at the top or bottom of each page; when you later edit that text the changes apply across the entire Web site. You can rearrange the structure of the Web site and FrontPage will update the hyperlinks. In short, using FrontPage to create a Web greatly automates and simplifies the process of developing and maintaining a Web site. In the next hands-on exercise you will create a complete Web site for T-Shirts To Go and then publish Janet Olson's personal pages to it. You will then publish the entire Web site to a floppy disk so that you can take it to any computer you use, and submit it to your instructor.

Top-down Design

Assume that T-Shirts To Go wants its Web site to showcase four product lines and the students who run the organization. Figure 9 shows the T-Shirts To Go Web site as it looks in Navigation view immediately after using the FrontPage Corporate Presence Web Wizard to develop the site. (The service pages will be changed to people pages in the hands-on exercise.) *Navigation view* displays the Web as an organization chart, and allows you to drag-and-drop pages to rearrange the structure of the Web site.

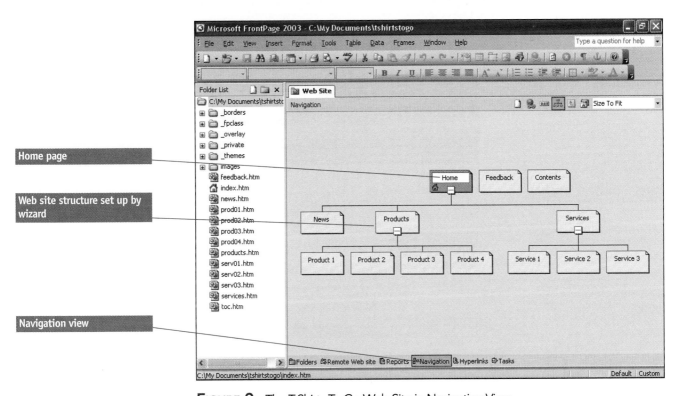

FIGURE 9 The T-Shirts To Go Web Site in Navigation View

Notice that the wizard uses generic page names such as Product 1, Service 1, and so on. You will edit these as you construct the site. Note also that the Folder list appears next to the Navigation view pane. For each page in the Web there is a corresponding icon in the Folder list, although the page names and file names are not necessarily the same. As you will see, FrontPage maintains the relationships between the various files by creating hyperlinks pointing to the appropriate file name. By default, FrontPage names the Web home page file either index.htm or default.htm, depending on the Web server that is available when you create the Web. In this case, the file is named index.htm.

Page Design

Once you have developed the basic structure of your Web site, you will begin designing and developing the individual pages. Figure 10 displays the home page mockup developed automatically by the Corporate Presence Wizard. Notice that the page is divided into three sections: a banner across the top of the page, a link bar at the left edge of the page, and a content area in the center.

Shared borders are used to display the banner and a link bar on each page in the Web. As the name implies, *shared borders* are standardized across pages, so each page has the same look and feel as the next. A *banner* is used to display standard content such as the name of the company and optional navigation buttons such as one for the site table of contents and feedback forms as shown in the figure. *Link bars* within the shared border(s) display buttons that help the user navigate to relevant areas of the site, typically to other pages at the same level, the previous page, and/or pages at the next level down.

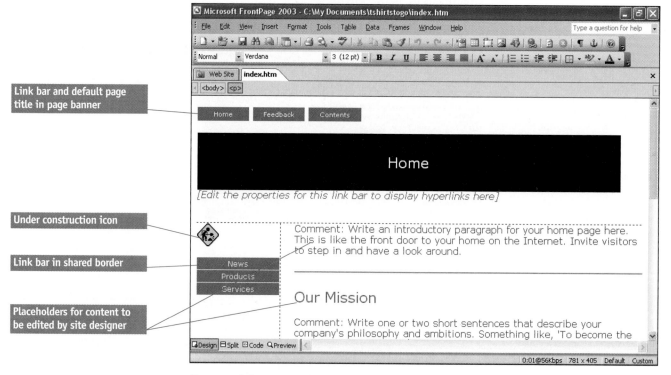

FIGURE 10 The Corporate Presence Home Page

You will substitute your own text for the page heading, content, and navigation buttons. Also, note the Under Construction icon that is the result of an option selected while running the wizard. This lets your intended audience know that you are still working on the content of the page. The other pages in the site are similar in design. You will enter content on each page to complete it. The wizard automatically defines the hyperlinks from the home page without your having to manually create the hyperlinks.

Figure 11a shows the home page of T-Shirts To Go as it will appear in Internet Explorer once the page is complete. As indicated, the text from the page layout mockup has been replaced by content relevant to T-Shirts To Go. Visitors will link to the products and/or people pages from the home page. Figure 11b shows the T-shirts product page (we removed the toolbars to show more of the page). It is a **child** of the home page; the home page is considered the **parent**. A T-shirt graphic was inserted, and the link buttons and page banner text were customized. The visitor can navigate throughout the site using the link bars which can be customized and which are updated by FrontPage as the designer changes the page names.

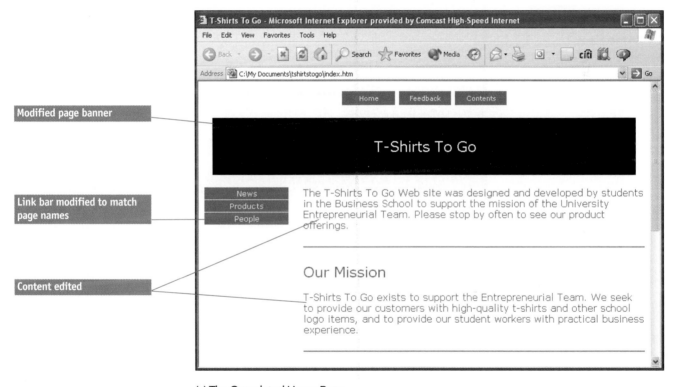

(a) The Completed Home Page

FIGURE 11   The T-Shirts To Go Web Site

WEB FILE NAMES

In order to insure that your Web site is compatible with as many types of computers as possible you should follow a few rules when naming your Web pages. Use lower case letters only, as some operating systems are case sensitive. Don't use special characters (*, #, and so on) other than the underscore character (_) in your file names.

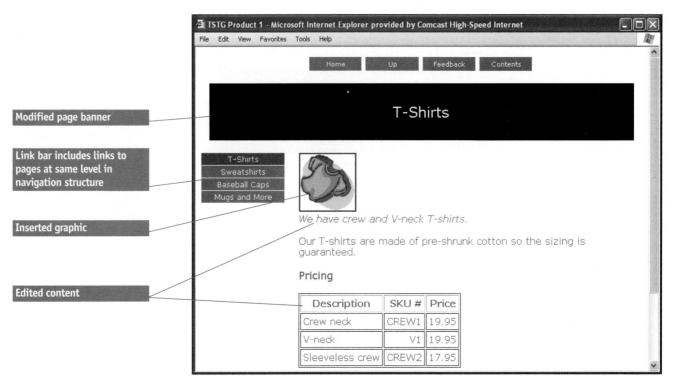

Modified page banner

Link bar includes links to pages at same level in navigation structure

Inserted graphic

Edited content

(b) The T-Shirts Products Page

FIGURE 11 The T-Shirts To Go Web Site (*continued*)

FRONTPAGE SERVER EXTENSIONS

The T-Shirts To Go Web site contains elements that must interact with a Web server to be fully functional. The feedback page that you will create while running the wizard is such a component. FrontPage Server Extensions must be installed on the Web server in order for the feedback page to work. Unfortunately, while you can view the feedback form in Design view in your Web, it will not be usable as we are publishing the Web to a disk, not a server with the FrontPage Server Extensions.

Publishing the Web Site

If you want to maintain all of the links, navigation structure, and so on created automatically by FrontPage, you cannot simply copy the site folder to a Web server. Instead, you must use the FrontPage *Publish Web command*, which transfers all the pages, images, folders, navigation structure, links, and so on to the designated *target*, or Web server that will receive the completed Web.

Many colleges and universities provide the possibility for students to create their own Web sites, store them on the campus Web server, and provide links to the student Web pages from the home page of the school. You need to investigate whether this is possible in your campus computing environment. Contact your instructor, your help desk, or your network center for instructions on how to do so.

Even if you cannot publish the T-Shirts To Go Web site to your school's Web server, you can publish it to a floppy disk, and that is the method we use in the hands-on exercise that follows shortly. Your published Web will not be accessible from the Internet, but you will be able to experience the Publish Web command and hand in the completed exercise to your instructor.

3   The Corporate Presence Web Wizard

Objective   To use a FrontPage Web wizard to create a simple Web site. Use Figure 12 as a guide in the exercise.

Step 1:   **Start the Corporate Presence Wizard**

■ Start FrontPage 2003, then pull down the **File menu** and select **New**. In the New task pane click **More Web site templates** to display the Web Site Templates dialog box in Figure 12a.

■ Click the **Corporate Presence Wizard icon**, then in the Options text box enter the location of the new Web site, **c:\My Documents\tshirtstogo** (with no spaces), or enter the folder name in which your instructor tells you to store the site. Click **OK** to begin the wizard.

■ At the first dialog box displayed by the wizard, read the introductory text and click **Next**. On the second wizard screen, select the options for **What's New**, **Products/Services**, **Table of Contents**, and **Feedback Form**. Deselect (uncheck) the other options. Click **Next** to continue.

■ On the next page select the topics **Mission Statement** and **Contact Information** for your home page, then click **Next**. On the next page of the wizard, check **Web Site Changes**, then click **Next** to continue.

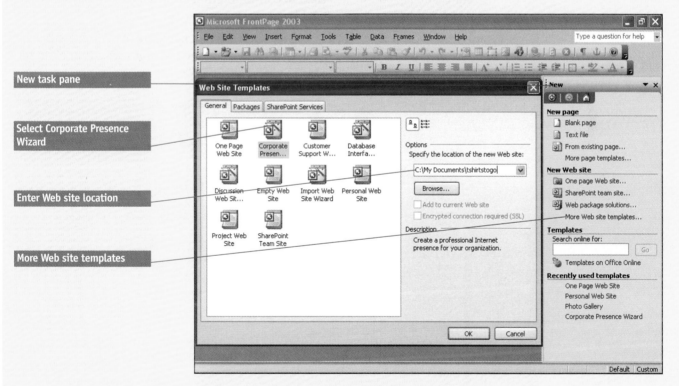

(a) Start the Corporate Presence Wizard (step 1)

FIGURE 12   Hands-on Exercise 3

Step 2: Create the Web Site

- Continuing with the wizard, enter **4** for the number of products, and **3** for the number of services you will link to from the relevant pages. Click **Next** to continue.

- On the next page, check the options **Product image** and **Pricing information** for the products pages. Uncheck all of the options for the service pages. Click **Next** to continue.

- The next page sets up the feedback form. Check **Full Name** and **E-mail Address**; uncheck the other options. Click **Next** to continue, then click **Next** again to store the feedback form in the default format.

- The next step defines options for the Table of Contents page. Select the **Keep page list up-to-date automatically** and **Use bullets for top-level pages** options. Click **Next** to continue.

- On the next page, select **Page title** and **Links to your main web pages** to appear at the top of each page. Select **E-mail address of your webmaster** and **Date page was last modified** to appear at the bottom of each page, then click **Next**.

- Click **Yes** to show the Under Construction icon on each unfinished page in the Web. Click **Next** to continue. Enter **T-Shirts To Go** as the full company name, enter **TSTG** as the short name, then enter a fictitious address including city, state, and zip code. Click **Next** to continue, enter fictitious phone numbers and e-mail addresses, then click **Finish**.

- FrontPage opens your site in Task view as shown in Figure 12b. If the Folder list is not visible, click the Folders button at the bottom of the window. Note the files that FrontPage has created. Close the folder list.

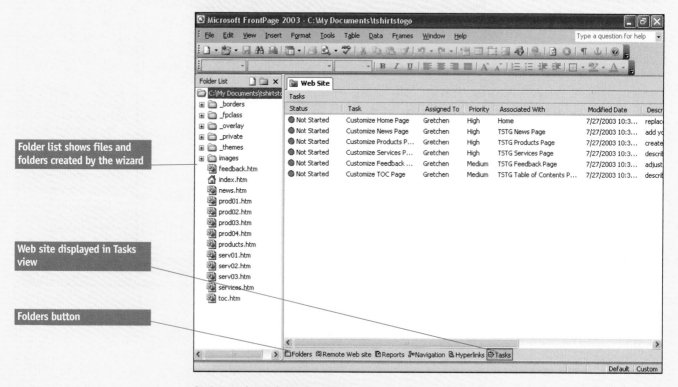

Folder list shows files and folders created by the wizard

Web site displayed in Tasks view

Folders button

(b) Create the Web Site (step 2)

FIGURE 12 Hands-on Exercise 3 (*continued*)

Step 3: **Assign Tasks**

- Our figure shows Gretchen assigned to complete all tasks, as she is the registered owner of FrontPage. (Your tasks may be assigned to someone else, or to no one.) Your pages are shown as tasks that are not yet started. When you return to the task list after modifying a page, it will show the status as In Progress.

- Double click the first task in the list, **Customize Home Page**. The Task Details dialog box in Figure 12c is displayed.

- Click in the **Assigned to text box** and substitute Janet Olson's name. Change the text in the **Description text box** as shown.

- Double click each task in turn and follow the same procedure to assign Janet and Beth the tasks in the list. Click **OK** after editing each task to return to Tasks view.

- After assigning the last task, right click the first task, then click **Start Task** in the shortcut menu to open the Web site home page. Note that the wizard applied the Journal theme as a default for the entire Web site.

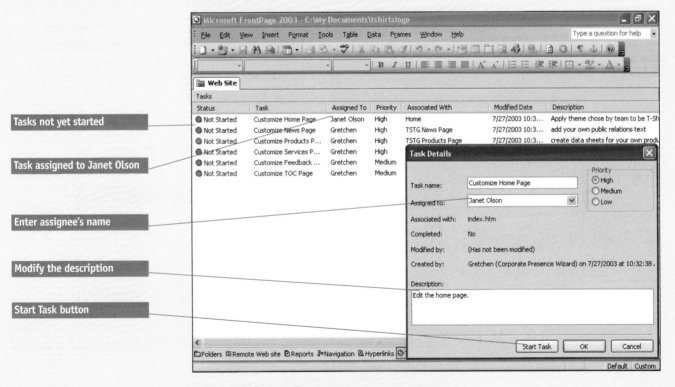

(c) Assign Tasks (step 3)

FIGURE 12 Hands-on Exercise 3 (*continued*)

SORT THE TASKS LIST

The Tasks List is initially sorted by task within priority; that is, high priority tasks are listed first, alphabetically by task description, then the medium priority tasks, and finally, the low priority tasks. You can change the sort order to show the Tasks List by status, priority, modify date, assigned to, and so on by clicking the column heading of any column. Click again and the sort order reverses from ascending to descending, or vice versa, depending on how it was sorted before you clicked.

Step 4: Edit the Page Banner

■ If necessary, pull down the **View menu** and select **Folder List** to see the folders and files that FrontPage has set up in your Web site. Click the down arrow in the **Toggle Pane button** on the Standard toolbar and select **Navigation Pane** to view the structure of your Web site as shown in Figure 12d.

■ Double click the **page banner** at the top of the page (where the word Home is displayed) to display the Page Banner Properties dialog box.

■ Change the entry in the Page banner text box to **T-Shirts To Go** as shown, then click **OK**. After a brief pause while FrontPage updates the Tasks List, hyperlinks, and so on, the new heading is displayed in the page.
   ❏ Note that this also changes the page title displayed in the title bar of your browser; that is, it modifies the <title></title> tag as you did in Code view.

■ Click the **Save button** on the Standard toolbar. A message is displayed asking if you want to mark the task as completed. Click **No** to save the Web and continue.

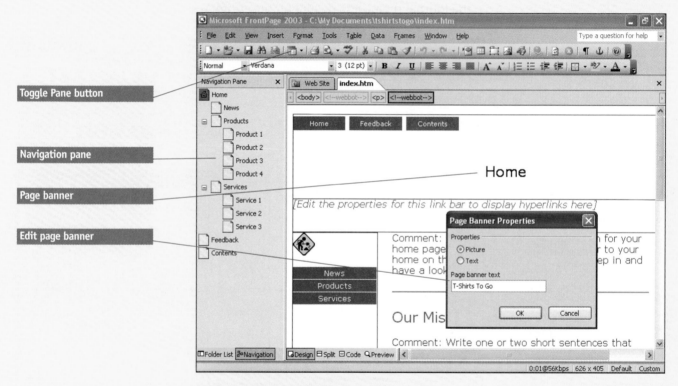

(d) Edit the Page Banner (step 4)

FIGURE 12   Hands-on Exercise 3 (*continued*)

THE NAVIGATION PANE

The Folder List displays all of the folders within your Web site, but does not indicate how they are related to each other in the Web. Click the down arrow in the Toggle Pane button on the Standard tool bar and select Navigation Pane to view the relationship between the various pages and folders in the Web.

Step 5: Modify the Page Content

- Close the Navigation pane to display more of the page. Click the line below the page heading as shown in Figure 12e (the page text is not yet modified), then press **Delete** to delete the place holder. Press **Delete** again to remove the blank line below the page heading.

- Click the first comment in the content section of the page and replace the existing text with the information shown in Figure 12e. Type the word **Entrepenurial** as shown. The FrontPage spell checker highlights the error. Right click the word and select **Entrepreneurial** from the shortcut menu to correct the error.

- Click the comment below the Mission Statement heading and revise the text as shown in the figure.

- Scroll down to view the contact information that was entered in the page by the wizard. Change the comment below the Contact Information heading to an appropriate sentence or two about contacting T-Shirts To Go.

- Click the **Save button** on the Standard toolbar. A message is displayed asking if you want to mark the task as completed. Click **No** to save the Web and continue.

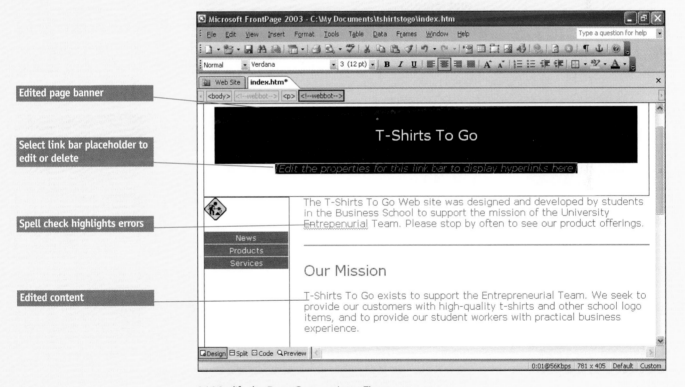

(e) Modify the Page Content (step 5)

FIGURE 12 Hands-on Exercise 3 (*continued*)

WEB PAGE DESIGN

The rule of thumb is to get your message across in one screen, as a significant number of surfers never go beyond the first page. Make it apparent how to access the rest of your Web from the home page, or your audience will move on before exploring your site.

Step 6: **Modify the Web Site in Navigation View**

- Pull down the **View menu**, then select **Navigation** to display the structure of the T-Shirts To Go Web site as shown in Figure 12f.
    - ❑ Note that the home page at the top of structure shows the name T-Shirts To Go (although you cannot see the entire name), not index.htm as it is named in the Folders list. This is a result of the change in the page banner that you made in Step 4.

- Click the **Portrait/Landscape button** on the Navigation toolbar to alter the layout.

- Click the **drop-down arrow** in the Zoom box on the Navigation toolbar and select **Size to Fit**. (This step may not be necessary now, but as the site gets larger it is a helpful shortcut to know.) Click the **Portrait/Landscape button** again to return to portrait layout.

- Right click the **Product 1 page** and select **Rename** from the shortcut menu, as shown in the figure. Enter the new page name **T-Shirts**, then press **Tab** to move the Product 2 page. You are in edit mode, as indicated by the blue highlighting of the page name. Change the name to **Sweatshirts**, then press **Tab** again and rename the Product 3 page **Baseball Caps**. Rename the Product 4 page **Mugs and More**.

- Right click the **Services page** one line below the home page to display the shortcut menu. Select **Rename**, then enter **People** as the new name of the page.

- Click the **Print button** on the Standard toolbar to print the T-Shirts To Go Web structure.

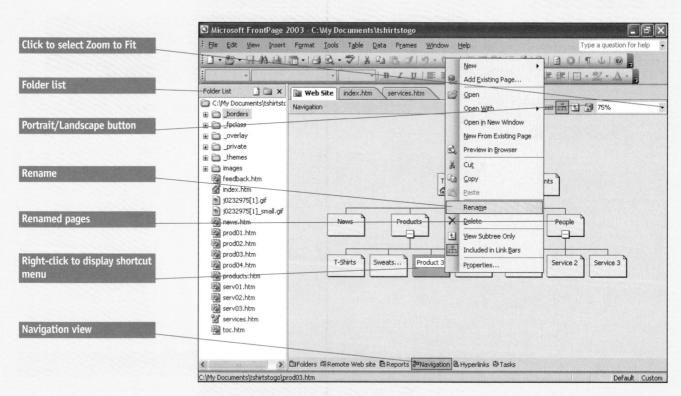

(f) Modify the Web in Navigation View (step 6)

FIGURE 12   Hands-on Exercise 3 (*continued*)

Step 7: **Complete the Home Page**

- Double click the **T-Shirts To Go home page** at the top of the Navigation structure to display the home page in Design view. The link bar at the left of the page has automatically changed to reflect the page name change from Services to People.

- Click the **Home, Feedback, and Contents link bar** at the top of the Web page to select it. Click the **Center button** on the Standard toolbar to center the buttons above the page banner.

- Click the **Under Construction icon** on the Link bar, then press **Delete** to remove the icon from the page. Press **Delete** again to remove the blank line and move the link bar to the top of the cell. Your page should be similar to the one shown in Figure 12g.

- Click the **Save button** on the Standard toolbar, then click **Yes** to indicate that the page is complete. Wait a few moments while FrontPage updates its files.

- Pull down the **View menu** and click **Tasks**. Note that the Customize Home Page task is shown as completed.

(g) Complete the Home Page (step 7)

FIGURE 12 Hands-on Exercise 3 (*continued*)

MODIFYING A THEME

To modify a theme, pull down the Format menu, select Theme, click the Modify button, and choose whether you are modifying colors, graphics, or text. Be aware however, that applying too many changes will defeat the purpose of themes, which is to tie your Web together with a common look.

Step 8: Add the Products

- Press **Ctrl+Click** to follow the Products link from the home page to display the main products page shown in Figure 12h. (We scrolled down in the page to display more of the page content.) Click the comment at the top of the page body and enter the text shown in the figure.

- Right click the text **Name of product 1**, then click **Hyperlink Properties** in the shortcut menu to display the Edit Hyperlink dialog box.

- Change the text to display to **T-Shirts** to match the dialog box, then click the **Screen Tip button** and enter the screen tip text as shown in the figure. Click **OK** to close the screen tip dialog box. Click **OK** again to close the Edit Hyperlink dialog box.

- Following the same steps, change the text of the three other product hyperlinks to **Sweatshirts**, **Baseball Caps**, and **Mugs**, **Water Bottles**, **and More**, respectively. Add appropriate descriptions below each hyperlink. Save the page.

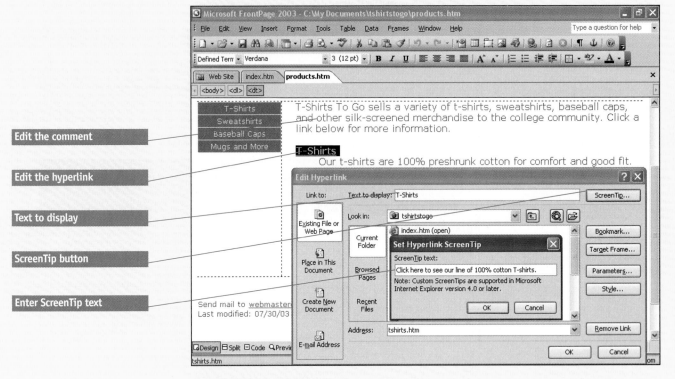

(h) Add the Products (step 8)

FIGURE 12   Hands-on Exercise 3 (*continued*)

SAVE CHANGES IN FRONTPAGE BEFORE PREVIEWING

When you open a page in Internet Explorer, it displays the page as it is stored on your hard drive. If you have just edited the page in FrontPage, but have not yet saved the page, the changes will not appear in your browser. Go back to FrontPage, save the page, then return to the browser window. Click the Refresh button and the browser will display the latest version of the page.

Step 9: Insert Graphics

■ Use **Ctrl+Click** to follow the **T-Shirts** hyperlink to the default Product 1 page created by the wizard. (Your page will not yet look like the figure.)

■ Pull down the **Insert menu** and click **Picture**, then click **Clip Art** to display the Clip Art task pane. Click **Clip art on Office Online** to open Internet Explorer.

■ Enter **shirt** in the search text box at the top of the Microsoft clip art page, then press **Enter** to search for shirt clip art.

■ Click the **Previous** and/or **Next** arrows at the bottom of the page to scroll through Microsoft's online graphics. When you find an appropriate image, right click it, then select **Copy** from the shortcut menu.

■ Click the **FrontPage icon** on the Windows taskbar to return to the T-Shirt page. Right click the **Product Image** placeholder, then select **Paste** from the shortcut menu and paste the image into your page as shown in Figure 12i. Close the Clip Art task pane.

■ Right click the image, then select **Auto Thumbnail** from the shortcut menu. Click the sizing handle at the lower right corner of the graphic, then click and drag to the upper left to reduce the size of the graphic.

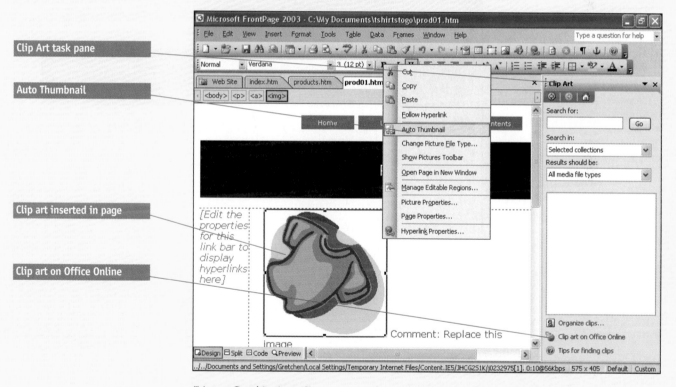

(i) Insert Graphics (step 9)

FIGURE 12 Hands-on Exercise 3 (*continued*)

FOUR WAYS TO CREATE HYPERLINKS

There are at least four ways to create a hyperlink in FrontPage. You can (a) pull down the Insert menu and select Hyperlink, (b) click the Insert Hyperlink button on the Standard toolbar, (c) right click the selected text and select Hyperlink from the shortcut menu, or (d) select the text for the hyperlink, then press Ctrl+K.

Step 10: Modify the Page

- Edit the page to include a description of the product, the different styles, and prices as shown in Figure12j. (We closed the toolbars to show more of the page.)

- Right click the link bar default text in the shared border at the left of the page and select **Link Bar Properties** from the drop down list to display the Link Bar Properties dialog box.

- Click the **Same level** option button to create a link bar to T-Shirts To Go's other products. Click **OK** to close the dialog box. The link bar is displayed in the shared border.

- Pull down the **File menu** and select **Save** (or click the **Save button** on the Standard toolbar). The Save Embedded Files dialog box is displayed. Click **OK** to save the graphic image with the page.

- Modify the other three product pages to include an image and product information. Save and close each page as you complete it. Do not close the Web site.

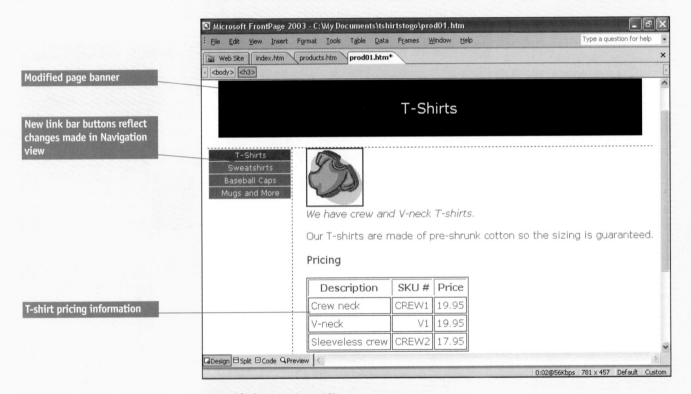

(j) Modify the Page (step 10)

FIGURE 12 Hands-on Exercise 3 (*continued*)

KEEP IT SIMPLE

Too many would-be designers clutter a page unnecessarily by importing a complex background, which tends to obscure the text. The best design is a simple design—either no background or a very simple pattern. We also prefer light backgrounds with dark text (e.g., black or dark blue text on a white background) as opposed to the other way around. Design, however, is subjective, and some people prefer the reverse. Variety is indeed the spice of life.

Step 11: Publish Janet Olson's Web Site

- Pull down the **File menu** and select **Open Site**. Click the down arrow in the **Look in text box** and navigate to Janet Olson's Web site. Select **jolsonweb**, then click **Open** to open the site.

- Pull down the **File menu** and select **Publish Site**, then click **Remote Web Site Properties** to display the Remote Web Site Properties dialog box in Figure 12k.

- Click the **File System option button**, delete any text in the Remote Web site location text box, then enter **c:\My Documents\tshirtstogo\jolson** to create a new folder in the T-Shirts To Go Web site.

- Click **OK** (not visible in the figure) to close the dialog box. FrontPage displays a message asking whether you would like to create a Web site at this location. Click **Yes** to display Remote Web site view (not visible in the figure).

- Click the **Publish Web site button** (at the bottom right of the window). The status bar indicates the progress of the publishing process.

- Click **Open your Remote Web site in FrontPage** (at the bottom left of the window). Janet Olson's home, travel, and embedded graphics pages should be displayed in the Web site tab.

- Double click **london.htm** to open the January travel page. FrontPage brought the pictures, captions, and descriptions with the photo gallery when the page was published.

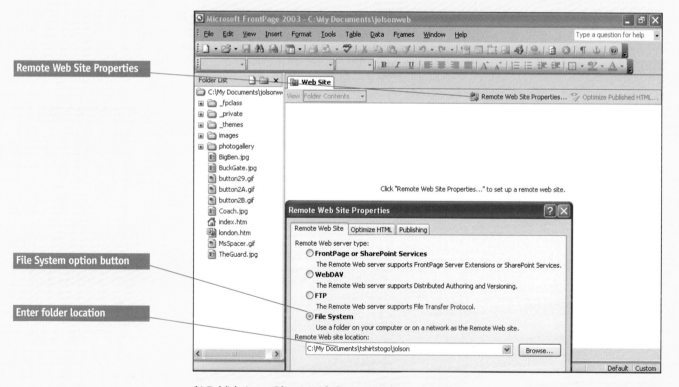

(k) Publish Janet Olson's Web Site (step 11)

FIGURE 12 Hands-on Exercise 3 (*continued*)

PUBLISHING VERSUS COPYING IN FRONTPAGE

When you copy a page from one Web site to another, the appropriate page references, hyperlinks, and so on, do not always copy properly and work in their new location. FrontPage will do the job much better for you when you use the Publish Selected Files command.

Step 12: Update the Site in Navigation View

- Pull down the **File menu** and select **Exit** to close Janet Olson's Web site within the T-Shirts To Go site and return to Janet Olson's stand-alone Web site. Pull down the **File menu** once again and select **Exit** to close this site. You should return to the T-Shirts To Go site. (If necessary, pull down the **File menu**, then select **Open Site** and reopen the T-Shirts To Go site as you normally would.)

- Click the **Web Site tab**, then click the **Navigation button** at the bottom of the window. If necessary, pull down the **View menu** and click **Folder List** so your FrontPage window matches Figure 12l. You should see the jolson Web site in the Folder list.

- Right click the **People page** and select **Add Existing Page** from the shortcut menu to display the Insert Hyperlink dialog box in Figure 12l.

- Click the down arrow next to the **Look in text box** and select **jolson**, then, if necessary click **Current Folder**. Scroll down in the list and select **index.htm**. Click **OK** to close the dialog box and create the link. Click the new page, **jolson/index**, in Navigation view, then press **F2** to edit the page name. Change it to **Janet Olson**.

- Double click the **People page** to open it. The link bar at the left of the page shows the link to Janet's page. Press **Ctrl+Click** to open Janet's home page. Pull down the **File menu** and select **Exit** to close Janet's home page.

- Click **serv01.htm** in the Folder list, then press and hold the **Shift key** while clicking **serv03.htm** to select three files, **serv01.htm**, **serv02.htm**, and **serv03.htm**. Press the **Delete key**, then click **Yes to All** to confirm that you want to delete the three files. (They were added by the wizard so you could see a larger site, but we don't need them now.)

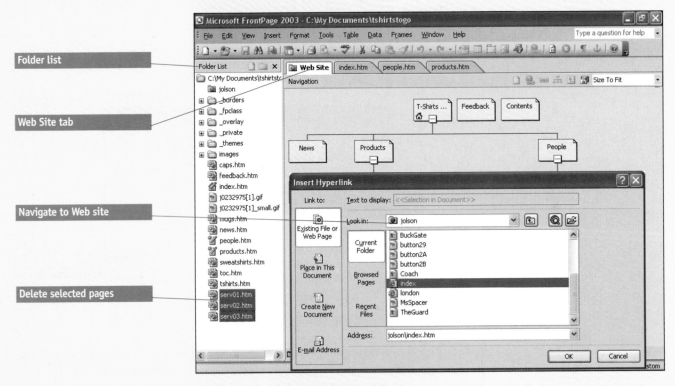

(l) Update the Site in Navigation View (step 12)

FIGURE 12 Hands-on Exercise 3 (*continued*)

Step 13:

Publish the Web Site

- Close all of the pages in the Web site, so that only the Web Site tab remains visible. Pull down the **File menu** and select **Publish Site** to display the Remote Web Site Properties dialog box.

- Click the **File System option button**, then clear the existing (default) text out of the Remote Web site location text box. Enter **a:** and click **OK**. (Check with your instructor to find out if there is a network folder that you should publish to instead of to the floppy.) Click **Yes** in response to message asking whether you want a new Web site at that location.

- FrontPage displays the Remote Web site view in Figure 12m. Click the **Publish Web site button** to begin the process.

- Click the **Ignore and Continue button** when you see the message indicating that some of the page elements will not work as they are not being published to a Web server running FrontPage Server Extensions or SharePoint Services.

- Click the **Ignore and Continue button** a second time when you see a message indicating that some private files are being published. FrontPage displays a status bar with time remaining as it publishes the Web site.

- Click **Open your remote Web site in FrontPage** to open the T-Shirts To Go site on the floppy disk, then click **index.htm** in the Folder list to open it and verify that FrontPage published the page. Close FrontPage.

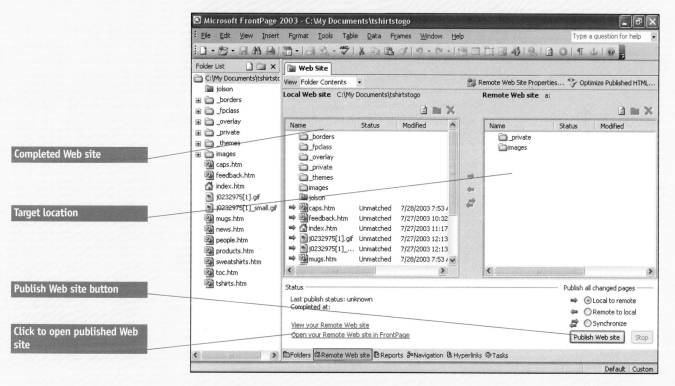

(m) Publish the Web (step 13)

FIGURE 12   Hands-on Exercise 3 (*continued*)

SUMMARY

To create a Web page, start FrontPage, then enter and format the text of the document in Design view. Or, if you prefer, use a wizard to create a page template with default content that you then edit. Microsoft FrontPage does the rest, generating the HTML tags needed to create the document and display it in a browser. Hypertext Markup Language (HTML) is the language used to create a Web page. HTML consists of a set of codes that format a document for display in a browser.

The Insert Hyperlink command is used to link a document to pages on another Web server, or within the same Web site. Hyperlinks may be inserted in the body of the document or in a link bar that is used for navigation within the Web site. Graphic images may come from a variety of sources and are inserted into a document through the Insert Picture command. FrontPage 2003 includes the Photo Gallery feature that allows you to create a Web page filled with photos. When you insert the pictures, FrontPage automatically creates a thumbnail image. You can add a caption to each picture if you wish.

A Web component can be inserted in a page to perform a predefined function such as maintaining a time stamp. A theme can be applied to one or more Web pages to create a unified look. Templates are used to simplify the creation of Web pages that require more complex formatting, such as columns and tables. Layout tables are used extensively within templates, and facilitate the creation of more complex documents. Shared borders are used to display link bars, page banners, hit counters, text, and images that are common to many (or all) pages on the Web. When content in a shared border is modified, the change is replicated throughout the Web.

Navigation and Folders views are used to maintain the Web site. File names, page titles, and page names should be changed to reflect the page content. FrontPage reports indicate broken links, pages that cannot be reached from other pages, and so on. They can be used to help manage your Web site.

FrontPage 2003 updates an internal database and indexes that record the structure of the Web site and relationships between the pages. Copying the Web does not preserve the FrontPage database and indexes that organize the Web. To maintain these elements of the Web, it should be published to the server using the Publish Web command. Even if a server is not available, it can be published to a local drive and tested. However, components such as a search form and hit counter that require the FrontPage Server Extensions will not work until they are published to a server running the extensions.

KEY TERMS

MULTIPLE CHOICE

1. Which of the following requires you to enter HTML tags explicitly in order to create a Web document?

   (a) A text editor such as the Notepad accessory
   (b) FrontPage
   (c) Both (a) and (b)
   (d) Neither (a) nor (b)

2. Which of the following is used to insert a time stamp in a FrontPage document?

   (a) The Time Stamp button on the Formatting toolbar
   (b) The Insert Component command
   (c) The Insert Date and Time command
   (d) All of the above

3. Which of the following is true about using a time stamp?

   (a) It is used to record the date a page was last visited
   (b) It is used to record the date a page was last modified
   (c) Both (a) and (b) above
   (d) Neither (a) nor (b) above

4. Which of the following views shows a list of items waiting to be completed in the current Web?

   (a) Tasks
   (b) Folders
   (c) Navigation
   (d) Links

5. The Format Background command:

   (a) Enables you to change the background color of a Web document
   (b) Cannot be used on the home page
   (c) Can only be used on the home page
   (d) Requires that you specify a graphic for the background

6. Which of the following can a hyperlink point to?

   (a) Another Web page at the current site
   (b) A different Web site
   (c) An e-mail address
   (d) All of the above

7. Which of the following codes creates a horizontal line across a page in an HTML document?

   (a) <hr>
   (b) <hl>
   (c) <p>
   (d) <ul>

8. How do you view the HTML tags for a Web document from within FrontPage?

   (a) Pull down the View menu and select the HTML command
   (b) Pull down the File menu, click the Save As command, and specify HTML as the file type
   (c) Click the Preview button on the Standard toolbar
   (d) Click the Code button at the bottom of the page in Page view

9. Where will the text enclosed in the <title> </title> tags appear when an HTML document is displayed using a Web browser?

   (a) In the title bar
   (b) At the beginning of the document
   (c) In the Folder list
   (d) All of the above

10. Which of the following statements regarding HTML tags is true?

    (a) They cannot be created in FrontPage
    (b) They cannot be viewed in FrontPage
    (c) They can be viewed from within Internet Explorer by clicking the HTML button
    (d) None of the above

11. Which of the following can you configure in a marquee?

    (a) The background color
    (b) The text color
    (c) Both (a) and (b)
    (d) Neither (a) and (b)

12. Which of the following can a FrontPage wizard include in a home page?

    (a) Page banner
    (b) Link bar
    (c) Shared borders
    (d) All of the above

... continued

multiple choice

13. Which of the following views displays the current Web as an organization chart?

   (a) Folders

   (b) Reports

   (c) Navigation

   (d) Tasks

14. Which of the following is a FrontPage feature used to lay out Web pages?

   (a) Hyperlinks view

   (b) A layout table

   (c) Tabs and indents

   (d) All of the above

15. Which default file name does FrontPage assign to a home page?

   (a) index.htm

   (b) home.htm

   (c) welcome.htm

   (d) None of the above

16. Which of the following can appear in a shared border?

   (a) Link bar

   (b) Graphic

   (c) Page title

   (d) All of the above

17. If you want the pages immediately below the current page to appear in a link bar based on your Web's navigation structure, which option would you specify?

   (a) Parent level

   (b) Back and next

   (c) Child level

   (d) Global level

18. Which of the following actions maintains FrontPage's internal database on links, navigation structure, and so on of your Web site?

   (a) Copying the Web site to a floppy disk

   (b) Copying the Web site to a Web server

   (c) Publishing the Web site to a Web server

   (d) Attaching a Web site to an e-mail message

19. Which view allows you to see what a page will look like in Internet Explorer?

   (a) Design view

   (b) Code view

   (c) Reports view

   (d) Preview view

ANSWERS

1. a	**8.** d	**15.** a
2. c	**9.** a	**16.** d
3. b	**10.** d	**17.** c
4. a	**11.** c	**18.** c
5. a	**12.** d	**19.** d
6. d	**13.** c	
7. a	**14.** b	

PRACTICE WITH FRONTPAGE

1. **Create Your Own Web Site:** At some point you will want your own personal Web site. FrontPage has a simple wizard to develop one.

   a. Open FrontPage, then pull down the File menu and select New to display the New task pane. Click More Web site templates, then click the Personal Web Site icon. In the textbox to specify the location of the new Web site, enter c:\My Documents\yournameweb (substituting your first initial, last name, such as gmarxweb, or use the location and Web site name given to you by your instructor. Click OK to begin the wizard.

   b. Double click index.htm to open the home page. Pull down the Format menu, then select Theme to display the Theme task pane. Select and apply a theme to your entire Web site (we chose Poetic) as shown in Figure 13. Scroll down in the page to view the standardized default content.

   c. Press Ctrl+Click on each hyperlink in the link bar at the left of the page to navigate around the site. Edit the content on each page (or as directed by your instructor), inserting photos in the photo gallery and adding hyperlinks on the favorites page. Save each page as you complete it.

   d. Publish the page to the T-Shirts To Go Web site you developed in the chapter, using first initial and last name as the folder name on the remote server, gmarx, for example. Follow the steps in Hands-on Exercise 3 if you need assistance. Add a hyperlink to the People page in the T-Shirts To Go Web site, following the instructions in Hands-on Exercise 3, Step 12 (substituting your name where appropriate) so that you appear as a student worker in the organization. Print the T-Shirts To Go Navigation view for your instructor as proof of completing this exercise.

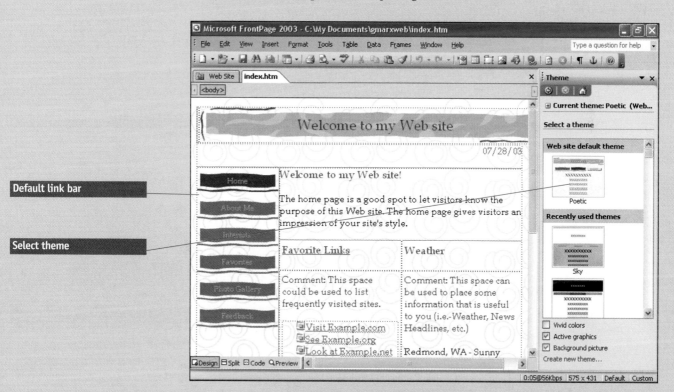

FIGURE 13 Create Your Own Web Site (exercise 1)

MODIFYING A FRONTPAGE WEB

When you create a Web in FrontPage, it keeps a database of all the page names and hyperlinks between pages. When you change the name of a page in Navigation view, FrontPage automatically updates any hyperlinks that refer to that page, thus greatly simplifying the maintenance of your Web site.

2. **View FrontPage Reports:** FrontPage maintains information about your Web site, that you can see in Reports view.

   a. Open the T-Shirts To Go Web site, then pull down the View menu and click the Reports button at the bottom of the window to display the Site Summary shown in Figure 14. Note the following statistics (yours may vary):

     ❏ The Web site contains a total of 82 files including buttons, link bars, and so on, in addition to the pages themselves. Despite this seemingly large number, the entire site is only 134 Kb in size and has no slow pages.

     ❏ The Web contains 143 hyperlinks created by the wizard or the designer, one of which is external, and three which are broken.

     ❏ There are five tasks major tasks remaining to be completed.

     ❏ One component is listed as having errors.

   b. Click **Broken hyperlinks** to view the errors. Click **Yes** if you want FrontPage to try to verify and fix the broken links, although be prepared for a short wait while it does so.

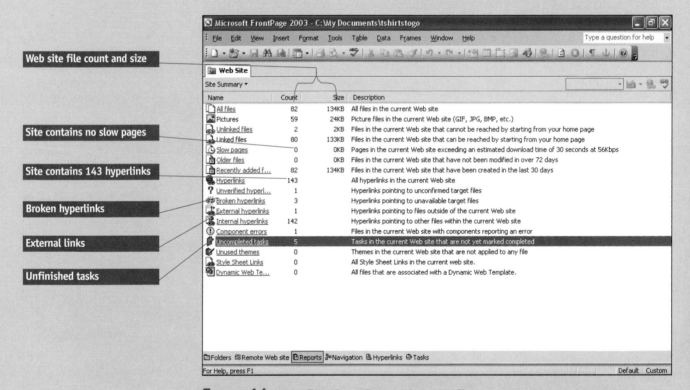

FIGURE 14   View FrontPage Reports (exercise 2)

CHECK FOR BROKEN LINKS

There is nothing quite as frustrating as finding a site that looks interesting, then discovering that some or all of the links are broken. The reports view in FrontPage will tell you which links are broken, including those that point to external Web pages. You should check your site periodically, or better yet, pull down the Tools menu and select Recalculate Hyperlinks to have FrontPage automatically repair them.

3. **Insert a Time Stamp and E-mail Link:** If the information on a page is relatively static, the person viewing it might wonder whether the information is still accurate or relevant. Your site visitors will appreciate knowing when you last updated your page, and how to contact you for information. If you develop a page using a template, a time stamp and an e-mail contact hyperlink may automatically be included. However, it is good to know how to create these elements. Hence, we show you how to add them.

a. Open Janet Olson's Web site. Click the Web site Tab, then double click london.htm to open the page. Click in the empty footer cell. Enter This page was last modified (include a space after the word *modified*) as shown in Figure 15.

b. Pull down the Insert menu and select Date and Time to display the dialog box in the figure (you will only see one dialog box at a time). Be sure the option button next to Date this page was last edited is selected. Select the desired date and time formats, then click OK. Enter a period after the date.

c. Press Enter to insert a new line below the Date/Time stamp. Enter You can contact me at jolson@bizschool.edu. When you press the space bar after the period, FrontPage automatically converts the e-mail address to a hyperlink.

d. Pull down the Format menu and select Paragraph to display the Paragraph dialog box in the figure. Be sure the line spacing is set to Single, then change the Before and After Spacing to 0. Click OK to close the dialog box. Save the page.

e. Click the Preview button at the bottom of the FrontPage window, then click the e-mail hyperlink you just created to display the New Message window in Outlook or your default e-mail editor. Close the message without saving or sending it. Pull down the File menu and select Close Site, then exit FrontPage.

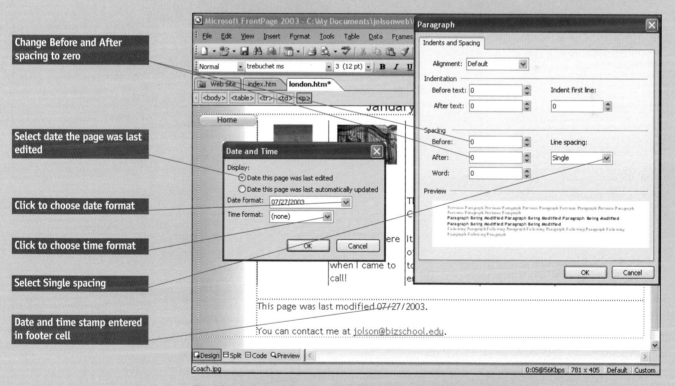

FIGURE 15 Insert a Time Stamp and E-mail Link (exercise 3)

4. **Create a Page Transition:** Similar to slide transitions in PowerPoint, you can create page transitions in FrontPage to add a special effect when opening a page.

   a. Open the page london.htm in Janet Olson's Web site that you created in Hands-on Exercise 2, then pull down the Format menu and select Page Transition. In the Page Transitions dialog box select the event (we chose Page Enter to have the transition take effect when the page is first opened), then select the duration (between 5 and 15 seconds is usually long enough to see the effect). Finally, select the transition effect that you want and click OK to save the transition. Save the page.

   b. Open the home page in Janet Olson's Web site, index.htm. Pull down the File menu, select Preview in Browser, then choose a screen resolution to open Janet Olson's home page within Internet Explorer.

   c. Click the travel link at the end of the first paragraph to open the January in London page. You will see the new page interwoven with and gradually displacing the original page, as shown in Figure 16.

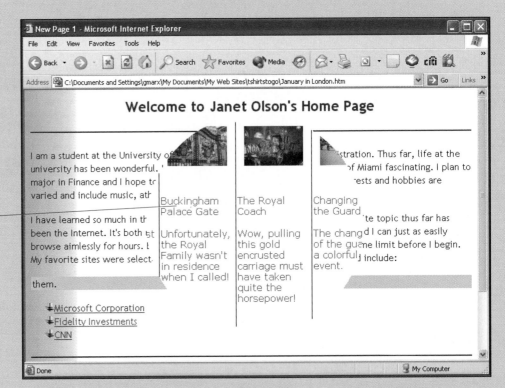

Travel page opening in Page Enter transition

FIGURE 16 Create a Page Transition (exercise 4)

GRAPHIC EFFECTS

Making your pages interesting is an important part of Web design. Marquees, page transitions, templates, animations, are all tools that a good designer will use. However, be sure that you are using them for a purpose, as you don't want your page to appear to be amateurish by inserting too many elements just to show that you know how.

5. **Create and Test a Hotspot:** You can create a clickable spot on a Web page by using the hotspot commands. Insert an image of the United States, for instance, in your page, then create a clickable region on the map to link to a corresponding page in your Web site. Want details on various features of a car? Create hotspots on the tires, the headlights, the roof rack, and so on. In short, you will find many uses for hotspots in your Web design.

a. Open the personal Web site that you created in Practice Exercise 1, then open the Interests page within the site. Pull down the Insert menu, select Picture, then select From File. Navigate to the folder where you unzipped the photos in Hands-on Exercise 2 (we used c:\Exploring Frontpage), select one of the photos, then click Insert. Right click the photo and select Auto Thumbnail from the shortcut menu.

b. Open Internet Explorer and enter www.expedia.com in the address bar. Click FrontPage on the Windows taskbar to return to your Web site.

c. Right click any visible toolbar and select Picture to display the Picture toolbar. Click the Rectangular Hotspot button and draw a rectangle over the thumbnail you just inserted in the page. The Insert Hyperlink dialog box in Figure 17 is displayed.

d. Click Browsed Pages to show recently visited sites on the Internet. Select the Expedia site. Click the Screen Tip button and enter a screen tip as shown in the figure. Click OK to close the Set Hyperlink Screen Tip box, then click OK again to close the Insert Hyperlink dialog box. Save the page.

e. Click the Preview button to view the page as it will appear in Internet Explorer, then hover over the image. The screen tip text is displayed. Click the link to display the Expedia page. Press Print Screen to make a screen image. Open Word and click Paste to paste the screen capture into a Word document. Write a short description of what you have accomplished, then print it for your instructor.

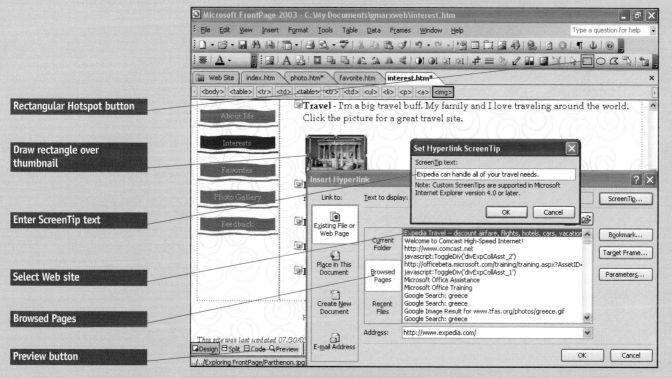

FIGURE 17 Create and Test a Hotspot (exercise 5)

MINI CASES

Designer Home Pages

Everyone has a personal list of favorite Web sites, but have you ever thought seriously about what makes an attractive Web page? Is an attractive page the same as a useful page? Try to develop a set of guidelines for a designer to follow as he or she creates a Web site, then incorporate these guidelines into a brief report for your instructor. Support your suggestions by referring to specific Web pages that you think qualify for your personal "Best (Worst) of the Web" award.

Employment Opportunities

The Internet abounds with employment opportunities, help-wanted listings, and places to post your résumé. Your home page presents your skills and experience to the entire world, and is an incredible opportunity never before available to college students. You can encourage prospective employers to visit your home page, and make contact with hundreds more companies than would otherwise be possible. Update your home page to include a link to your résumé, and then surf the Net to find places to register it.

Forms in HTML Documents

Many Web pages require you to enter information into a text box, then submit that information to a Web server. Every time you use a search engine, for example, you enter key words into a form that transmits your request to the search engine. Another common form is a guest book where you register as having visited the site. Including a form on a page is not difficult but it does require additional knowledge of FrontPage. Open FrontPage Help and search on the keyword Form to see what you can find about forms, then summarize your results in a brief note to your instructor.

Publishing Your Web Page

In the chapter you published a Web site to disk using the FrontPage Publish Web command. You may or may not be able to use this command to publish your Web site to your campus Web server. Contact your Help Desk or Web master and find out whether you can publish directly from FrontPage. If not, find out what the appropriate procedure is and write up a short description for your instructor.

Add Your Home Page to the Yahoo Catalog

After you have completed your home page and your Web master has placed it on the college Web server, you want others to be able to find it. You can add your page to various catalogs such as Yahoo. Go to docs.yahoo.com/info/suggest/ to find out how to suggest a link to your site within the Yahoo search engine. Write a short memo to your instructor explaining the process.

Experiment with the Photo Gallery

Open the london.htm page you created in Hands-on Exercise 2. Right click the photo gallery, and select Photo Gallery Properties from the drop-down menu to display the Photo Gallery Properties dialog box. Select a picture, then click Edit. Explore the options on the Edit Picture dialog box, such as rotating and cropping a picture, and changing its size.

Index

M

Make Column Autostretch, 15
Marquee Properties dialog box, 10
marquees, 2
    continuous marquees, 10
    inserting, 10
multimedia files, 19

N–O

Navigation command (View menu), 32
Navigation Pane, 30
Navigation view, 32
    updating Web sites, 38
nested tags, 3
New command (File menu), 6, 27
New Photo Gallery dialog box, 20
numbered lists, 2

Open Site command (File menu), 17

P

page banners, editing, 30
Page Properties dialog box, 11
Page Transition command (Format menu), 46
pages. *See* Web pages
Paragraph command (Format menu), 45
Paragraph dialog box, 45
parent pages, 25
photo gallery, 16
    creating, 20
    publishing, 16
    thumbnails, 20
Picture command (Insert menu), 20, 35, 47
pictures. *See* graphics
pixels, 15
place holders, deleting, 31
Preview in browser command (File menu), 14
Preview view, 2
previewing Web pages, 2, 14
Publish Selected Files command, 37
Publish Site command (File menu), 37, 39
Publish Web command, 26
publishing
    local area networks (LANs), 22
    photo galleries, 16
    Web sites, 26, 37, 39

R

Remote Web Site Properties dialog box, 37, 39
Remote Web site view, 39
repairing hyperlinks, 44
reports, 44

Reports command (View menu), 44
rules. *See* horizontal lines

S

Save command (File menu), 7, 36
Save Embedded Files dialog box, 21
saving changes, 34
selecting text, 7
servers. *See* Web servers
shared borders, 24
sites. *See* Web sites
sorting Tasks Lists, 29
source code, 3. *See also* HTML
    viewing, 12
Standard toolbar, 4
    displaying, 6
Start button, opening FrontPage, 6

T

Table menu commands
    Layout Table, 18
    Table Properties, 21
tables
    editing cell properties, 21
    page layout, 18
tags. *See* HTML
targets, 26
Task Details dialog box, 29
task pane, 4
    Layout Tables and Cells, 15
Tasks Lists, 29
Tasks command (View menu), 33
templates, 15. *See also* wizards
    modifying, 18
    opening, 17
testing hyperlinks, 8, 22
text
    formatting, 3, 9
    marquees. *See* marquees
    selecting, 7
Theme command (Format menu), 13, 43
themes, 2, 4–5, 13
    customizing, 13
    modifying, 33
thumbnails, 16, 20
    Auto Thumbnail command (shortcut menu), 35
time stamps, 16
    inserting, 45
titles
    page titles versus file names, 14
    title tag, 3
toolbars, 4–5
    displaying, 6
Toolbars command (View menu), 6
transitions, 46

U–V

W–Z